Bits of Psyche

This book includes material from Michael Eigen's celebrated and long-running seminar series, to explore some of the classic and contemporary key concepts in psychoanalytic theory and practice.

Drawing on the work of Winnicott, Bion and Lacan, Eigen explores key psychoanalytic themes which have risen to prominence over the last decade such as the place of politics in psychoanalysis, life, death and psychic deadness, and the role of lies and deception in the consulting room and our world.

With over 50 years of experience in leading seminars and working psychoanalytically, Eigen's work is essential reading for all psychoanalysts and psychoanalytic psychotherapists.

Michael Eigen is a psychologist and psychoanalyst from the USA. He is the author of 30 books and numerous papers. He has given a private seminar on Winnicott, Bion, Lacan and his own work since the 1970s. Eigen is known for his work with patients "who had been given up on by others", including people who experience psychosis.

Bits of Psyche

Selected Seminars by Michael Eigen

Michael Eigen

Routledge
Taylor & Francis Group

LONDON AND NEW YORK

Designed cover image: Melanie W. Cohen

First published 2024
by Routledge
4 Park Square, Milton Park, Abingdon, Oxon OX14 4RN

and by Routledge
605 Third Avenue, New York, NY 10158

Routledge is an imprint of the Taylor & Francis Group, an informa business

© 2024 Michael Eigen

British Library Cataloguing-in-Publication Data
A catalogue record for this book is available from the British Library

Library of Congress Cataloguing-in-Publication Data
Names: Eigen, Michael, author.
Title: Bits of psyche : selected seminars by Michael Eigen / Michael Eigen.
Description: 1 edition. | New York, NY : Routledge, 2024. |
Includes bibliographical references and index. |
Identifiers: LCCN 2023044852 (print) | LCCN 2023044853 (ebook) |
ISBN 9781032658933 (hardback) | ISBN 9781032674308 (paperback) |
ISBN 9781032658926 (ebook)
Subjects: LCSH: Psychoanalysis. | Psychoanalysis--Political aspects. |
Psychoanalysis and culture. | Psychotherapy--Case studies.
Classification: LCC BF109.E54 E54 2024 (print) | LCC BF109.E54 (ebook) |
DDC 150.19/5--dc23/eng/20231218
LC record available at https://lccn.loc.gov/2023044852
LC ebook record available at https://lccn.loc.gov/2023044853

ISBN: 978-1-032-65893-3 (hbk)
ISBN: 978-1-032-67430-8 (pbk)
ISBN: 978-1-032-65892-6 (ebk)

DOI: 10.4324/9781032658926

Typeset in Sabon
by MPS Limited, Dehradun

Contents

Foreword

Many years ago, Alan Watts, Henry Elkin (Eigen's main analyst) and Michael Eigen were in a car together going to an event. Watts and Elkin were in the front seat with Eigen in the back. Alan Watts, during a conversation, remarked to Henry Elkin that there is a huge difference between the spoken word and the written word. These seminars were transcribed word for word and then edited. There is nothing like the live, spoken, spontaneous word, especially coming from Michael Eigen in his New York City office. These transcribed seminars come close, but the sensory input is missing. Eigen's tone, inflection and physical movements when speaking, unfortunately, are not represented in these pages. For example, sometimes when he speaks passionately, he taps his feet to the rhythm of his words. Sometimes, while speaking, he startles everyone by raising his voice suddenly and dramatically to make a point because he feels so passionately. The environment and background feeling of Eigen's live New York seminars go beyond the ability to capture in the written word.

Included in this book are seven edited seminars which give a flavor of the Tuesday group topics and Eigen's breadth of knowledge. Threads of Eigen's inner essence run through his work and these seminars are no exception. Attending and participating in his seminars produces feelings beyond words. Jim Nicholls once remarked that it is like attending Church, meaning the spiritual feelings run through you. I think he is right. Something takes hold and one softens, and comes away with renewed hope in humanity, in one's self. Eigen's seminars provide a welcoming haven from the storm, if only for a little more than an hour each week. The cumulative effect of spiritual, educational and transformative growth bears fruit in touching ways. Psychological incubation comes to mind.

As you read, try to imagine the background noise of the Upper West Side streets. Often school groups of children pass by laughing and talking. Babies and toddlers cry and scream. Traffic hums along, with people talking as they walk on the sidewalks outside his first-floor office. Of course, New York City would not be complete without the sirens of police or ambulances whirling by. We were treated to all of these sounds and more, with Eigen's windows slightly cracked open, while the blinds were closed.

Often, I would think about the topic Mike would be discussing and the emotions it would stir inside of me, juxtaposed against the backdrop of emotional life that was streaming into the office from the outside.

It was not always this way. Eigen was on the 14th floor of the same building for many years before moving to the first floor. Prior to that, he held his Tuesday seminar on West 90th Street near Riverside Drive. In the late 1970's he moved to his current building.

Over the years, during my tenure with the group, many people dropped in from around the world and the United States. That is how Eigen ran it, casual, informal and without any pressure or expectations. Often, people were greeted with an enthusiastic hello and when departing, many hugs from Eigen were shared. Ofra Eshel, Annie Reiner, Joe Burke, Michal Heiman, Shalini Masih, Jim Nicholls and many more dropped in during the close to fifteen years I was privileged to attend in person before the Pandemic began. Of course, there were the regulars, some of whom stayed many years and some who stayed for a little while before moving on.

For the last three-plus years, the Tuesday group has moved online, with its own tone and rhythm that is different from in person with Eigen. It misses the laid-back feeling of being in New York, but has brought together people who would not have been able to have the experience of the Tuesday seminar at all. The seminars in these pages are a mix of in-person and online seminars.

It's amazing to contemplate that this group has been ongoing for over fifty years. Some people have been there since the beginning and as life is life, some have passed away, too. Through it all, Eigen has adapted to the situation and taken it all in stride. I think about people who passed through, before my time, and wonder what it would be like if the time-space continuum made an exception and brought all who have attended over the years together, just once.

One could say that Eigen links us all, but really, it's also the structure of our existence that brings us together to experience and learn about the human spirit, not only through the lens of Eigen's view, but also through the experience itself, being together in support and reverie.

Keri Cohen

Introduction

The human psyche doesn't stop – pulse beats, drum beats, mega and mini-beats, internal-external wars, creativity, interweaving of capacities, mixtures of all sorts with more than dashes of wonder. Real horror is horrible yet we have entertaining horror fiction and art. Whatever disturbs also turns into a myth that structures and magnifies. Bion felt war tries to make us see what is inside of us through the enactment of destructive forces echoed by great writings throughout history. And yet a sense of beauty permeated his life and his last talks underlined beauty in psychoanalysis.

This is a book of seven seminars I gave between 2015 and 2022, four explicitly related to Bion's work (Chapters 2, 4, 6, 7). Chapter 1 focuses on the vicissitudes of trauma and Chapters 3 and 5 on vicissitudes of shame. It is a paradox of our beings that so much aliveness has to do with death. It is well known that as Freud's work developed interplay of life and death forces gained emphasis. Psychic deadness became a theme of existential literature as part of the aftermath of wars and also became a theme of significant areas of psychoanalytic work. It can be a worthwhile experience to keep a kind of diary charting moments of aliveness-deadness throughout the day or lifetime – so many kinds of aliveness and deadness. Death-rebirth mythologies echo moments of experience throughout life (Eigen, 1996, 2021). Joy gains part of its intensity, opening and renewal against this backdrop.

Chapter 1 is entitled "Dread, Dead, Deflected and Little Bits of Grace." It is based on a seminar given in 2015 on "Trauma Clots" Chapter 4 in *Feeling Matters* (2007). It is on a particular class, September 25 in an ongoing series and a particular patient we are calling Arnie. It touches ins and outs of trauma tracing aspects of origins, outcomes and unknown quandaries. One of our main interests is the life of trauma, its interactions with individual, group, society, positive-negative aspects in areas of destruction and growth. There is such a thing as generative destruction and destructive generativity, mix-ups profound and baffling. As I wrote in an earlier work (2018), the challenges of being human are immense. In certain ways, Arnie came to associate pockets of deadness in himself

DOI: 10.4324/9781032658926-1

with areas of deadness in his mother. But that is only the beginning, so much more is needed for psychic growth and something in Arnie pushed him toward greater openness. In speaking about Arnie we open discussion about wider human culture, including our perception and use of forces in nature. Emphasis here is not so much "solving" puzzles but creating conditions for the growth of experiencing.

Chapters 2, 4, 6 and 7 were seminars working with Bion's *A Memoir of the Future* (1991). I write "working with" rather than "focused on" because passages from many parts of Bion's life and work make their appearance adding to a rich tapestry woven through nearly forty years of his writings. Chapter 2 is titled "Bits of Bion and Multiple Undercurrents" given December 5, 2017 close to the end of Trump's first year as President. Chapter 4 is "After the Election: Between Truth and Lies and More" December 15, 2020 a month after Biden's election. Chapter 6 is "Playing with Bion: Gifts and Dreads of Our Problematic Psyche" December 21, 2021. Material for Chapter 7: "Bits of Madness" was given in one of my private seminars June 2022 and further developed for the International Bion Conference Mexico 2022 November 10–13. The version given here combines both in an updated edit. The Association sponsoring this talk was A-SANTAMARIA PSICOANALISIS MEXICO A.C.

The character Rosemarie in *A Memoir of the Future* remarked "And now the mind has become available for the extension of lies, deceptions, evasions, to produce bigger, better liars and cheats than any 'human' mind had so far achieved." (p. 129) We have come a long way from Bion's admiration of Keats's "man of achievement" one who has the capacity to live in ambiguities. H. L. Mencken was not quite up to snuff when he predicted that someday the American soul would get what it wants and elect a moron for a president. He did not quite reach Rosemarie's dictum made forty years later and Rosemarie's reflection came about forty years before Trump became president. Lies tend to foreclose ambiguity, at least as used at this moment in our political world. It is no accident that the seminars chosen here range from the year before Trump was elected to the current moment, the middle of Biden's presidency so far.

Many respect Bion as a seeker of deep truth but truth can take many forms and Bion is a spokesperson, among much else, for the truth of human imagination. He points out Freud's use of ancient drama as a model for psychic realities, e.g., the "Oedipus Complex" from Sophocles Oedipal trilogy. Freud himself told us literary writers are companions of psycho-analysis, both expressing emotional truths. Bion describes his trilogy, *A Memoir of the Future* (1991), written in the 1970s, as psychoanalytic fiction or fiction expressing truth(s) of psychoanalysis. In *Memoir* an unknown enemy seeks to overturn personality and social structures. In a gesture that apes Saint Matthew's testament that "the last shall be first and first last" Alice, the head of a landed estate becomes Rosemarie's servant, a reversal of roles. The coming of a nameless enemy throws the gentry into chaos as it disperses into the countryside hiding.

Many of the characters discover they are fiction more real than real-life people. But the discovery goes both ways as we come to see fictional aspects of our identities. A character called Myself, a semi-representation of the character Bion's inner experience, says at one point, "... the dialogue between me and me might just as well be conducted between me and a fictitious character." (p. 113) And again Myself explicitly states, "I am also a fictitious character." (p. 130) In varied ways, Bion brings out a fictional sense of human identity.

Another theme is Bion's valuation of what I tend to call the creative unknown. I think of a saying by Eddington, "Something unknown is doing we don't know what." Bion so respected the unknown in psychoanalysis that he developed the formula F in O to express a kind of faith in unknown, perhaps unknowable reality, in a therapy session, especially unknown emotional reality. By faith, he did not mean belief but an open attitude he sometimes described as being without memory, understanding, expectation or desire – a radical openness to the unknown of the moment. Sometimes his depictions make me think of Saint Paul who said "God is love" and added, "What a dreadful thing to fall into the hands of the living God." How much life can we take, how much aliveness and what kind can we sustain or tolerate in what ways? Bion writes of catastrophic dread as a link that holds personality together. He also wrote of positive-destructive aspects of love, hate and knowledge links. As his work unfolded a kind of Faith became a deeply unifying dimension.

In *Memoir* many characters make appearances giving expression to multiple aspects of our beings. We have touched several of a number of significant themes here in the introduction developed in the chapters ahead. It is of interest to point out that the first of Bion's books was on group experience and this last extended work reflects individual and group dynamics in complex, imaginative and real ways.

Chapter 3 is called "Tiny I-Bits and Big Ones Too" and focuses on Chapter 6 "Shame" in *Sense, Infinities and Everyday Life* (2015). The seminar was given in 2018. Chapter 5 is titled "A Near Christmas Meeting" given a few days before Christmas 2020. The two seminars on shame span Trump-Biden moments and while touching ancient themes open current questions and dilemmas. God asked Adam why he was hiding and Adam confessed his shame. It's hard for me to resist playing with parts of this word it is so packed with nuances: Sh. Sham, ham, me. Something went wrong in the Garden and continues its work in the current moment. Again the word current: many currents flowing in many directions as well as getting stuck in all kinds of ways.

I began giving private seminars over 50 years ago, first on Winnicott and eventually adding Bion, Lacan and my own work. I met Winnicott in 1968 and Bion 1977. Both have added immeasurably to my life – and that is an understatement. In recent years my weekly seminars focused mainly on Bion's *A Memoir of the Future* and my own work, alternating every several weeks. I'd say alternating currents but the currents are all mixed up and create mixtures of their own. I am grateful to Keri Cohen for urging me to make a book of some of them. She played an important role in this selection, which spans the past seven years, a vital historical moment when so many values are challenged, reversed and turned upside down. Thanks, also, to Victoria Willis and Irit Davidovich for transcriptions of these seminars although I am mainly responsible for their editing.

One of Bion's characters called God imaginary and creative activity imaginary too - but here we are, an imaginary book ready to go into real print and touch whoever it can, hopefully in helpful ways. Bion posits a destructive force that keeps on working but he also deeply affirms what he calls F in O, reality that keeps opening and opening our beings.

References

Bion, W. R. (1991). *A Memoir of the Future*. London: Routledge.

Eigen, M. (1996). *Psychic Deadness*. London: Routledge.

Eigen, M. (2007). *Feeling Matters*. London: Routledge.

Eigen, M. (2015). *Image, Sense, Infinities and Everyday Life*. London: Routledge.

Eigen, M. (2021). Rebirth: It's Been Around a Long Time. Eds. K. Fuchsman and K. Cohen. *Healing, Rebirth and the Work of Michael Eigen: Collected Essays on a Pioneer in Psychoanalysis*. London: Routledge.

Chapter 1

Dead, Dread, Deflected and Little Bits of Grace

[Working with Chapter 4, "Trauma Clots" in *Feeling Matters* 2015]

We reached dread and dead linked to a death spot in Arnie's mother. We talked about his children getting flattened out by being functional, a kind of paradox. You have to open up to see that someone could be flattened out and live a less satisfactory life in certain ways and still have a rich life in other ways. I think of the so-called "operational personality" described in France, of people with an impoverished feeling succeeding in high places, an exaggerated version of losing an affect to survive and do well. Arnie's children actually had good lives in spite of their parents (as well as because of). They had productive lives and real problems, gains, losses, a price to pay. Part of ancient wisdom is that you have to give something up, lose something, to survive, or more deeply, "lose yourself to find yourself."

When I was young there was a current in the field that felt one had to be well analyzed in order to build a less self-destructive life. You were even warned not to make big decisions until the analysis was well underway. That might be true for some, but don't go into analysis thinking the mess of life is going to be "solved" – and certainly not "dissolved." You live with the mess you are or you don't live at all. Maybe wisdom glimpses will help you work with the mess better. You might even become, in some ways, a better-quality mess. I think of Samuel Beckett, a patient of Bion's when they were younger: "Fail. Fail again. Fail better." Actually, the quote is "Try again. Fail again. Fail better." But I could not resist starting with failure, so close to the Fall that is part of *Genesis* or the Hebrew, *Berashis* ("In the beginning"). The fall is associated with beginnings, genesis, creativity. It does not hurt to add the final s is often pronounced t. Life as we know it is a combination of high, low and everything between.

Don't expect to say "Bye-bye mess," and that's that. But you may be surprised by a sense of "new beginnings" (Balint, 1956) pervading existence as well as the apple stuck in one's throat. Every mess you leave, another comes up. Sometimes I almost feel the diminishing mess welcomes the somewhat new version.

In the session I'm thinking about, Arnie was talking about his children and I was surprised to hear about the dead mother part inside his baby self.

DOI: 10.4324/9781032658926-2

He had idealized his mother as part of his life and kept making excuses for her. He could not face the fact that her depression was tied to parts of himself dying or not coming alive, lacking support to sustain life. For me, it was a welcome sign to see him see his mother more as she was rather than as he made her up. It's not simply that idealization covers the negative to keep hope alive. It can also paralyze the development of complex perceptions of difficult realities, leading to areas of psychic paralysis. In Arnie's case, it led to feeling stuck inside a stillbirth that could not happen. There were times he would say, "I see my mother, I see my mother." He would feel her coming alive inside him only to fall back into a birth that could never happen, smothered by a sense of damage.

Now he spoke more about his mother's depression. He used to speak about how it came out of the blue, precipitated by moving from her home in the south to New York City, a whole new world that overwhelmed her. He felt events caused her depressive periods, her husband's death, children leaving home. When she was permanently hospitalized in his twenties, he rationalized it thinking that changes in life were too much for her. Now he was beginning to get deeper inklings: "My God! I grew up with a depressed mother! And I'm depressed! I didn't understand why I had depressive breakdowns. When my children were born, I broke down. I broke down when my grandchildren were born and it was not just because my mother became permanently hospitalized when I was twenty years old. There's some kind of link between birth and breakdown, birth and depression.

"A book you told me about is beginning to sink in (Bloch, 1977). It's not just her depression that made me afraid of her dying. It made *me* afraid of dying. I mean – we are all afraid of dying but this is something more. It's as if parts of me were partly dead because she could not nourish them. I was dying as a person in little and big ways." He was letting more of himself in, more of his mother in, more psychic reality in. It can be a lot to let even a little more reality in.

His insight flow continued. "All my life I thought or tried to convince myself she was "normal" and her breakdowns were aberrations. I would feel I could make her better – that I *should* be able to make her better. That it was somehow my fault and that if I acted better she would be better. But I could not make her be what she was not and continued to suffer her put-downs, disparagement, blame, as if I were always failing. I think now I came to feel I was some kind of essential failure because I could not make my mother appreciate me. Any good word she managed was followed by some kind of depreciation. Depreciation rooted deeply in her nature."

Arnie insisted for years that she was normal when he was young. And there may have been some part of her that could have nourishing moments. It is not so unusual for someone to be capable of nourishing moments and crazy other moments. One can be nourishing and depriving at the same time. I've known a good number of people who felt they had two different sets of parents when they were growing up, the good ones and the awful ones. It can make it confusing to be with people never knowing which one is going to show up. Relationships are challenges. I suspect one of the real benefits of therapy is making room for spectrums of possibilities, so many different aspects of self with a place to go. People can make your head spin but nowhere near the ways you spin your own. When marriage works, part of the benefit is learning to work with impossibilities that support possibilities. So often we hallucinate solutions where difficulty continues but we grow from catching on to ourselves and others and appreciating what we share and go through.

As he began to take in the depth and extent of his mother's depression he almost felt normal by comparison or, at least, that he was not as violently and extensively depressed as she. She was permanently hospitalized. So far that is not the case with Arnie and I doubt it will be. He may have suffered breakdowns but he sought help and continues to work with life's challenges day to day. To be depressed is one thing, to suffer permanent hospitalization is another. People are so variable. Some may suffer from psychosis and still function well in the outside world; others may need lifelong care. One can be quite mad and be president of the United States. There are many ways to mix sanity and madness.

When Arnie was in his twenties he would visit his mother in the hospital, and she would try to have sex with him. In a way, depression can be a kind of plug. Pull the plug and all kinds of things come out. What is dead? What is alive?

Arnie envisions a deadness in his mother exacerbating baby dread. Why would deadness make a baby afraid? You can answer for yourself. It's dreadful to be with a dead mother, a mother whose dead spot is touching, animating, stimulating this dread. A dread that is horrifyingly alive. Maternal depression stimulates a baby's fear of death. It may be for a baby so much is alive, animate, and here comes this dead-dread spot stimulating psychic death. Later on, you will discover actual death. There are, as has often been said, many ways to die. And live. A counterpart corollary is Saint Paul's sober outcry, "It is a dreadful thing to fall into the hands of the Living God." The very intensity of life is threatening.

So who's dead? Arnie's mother? Arnie? Can depression sometimes (often) be a dampening of dread? Bion (1970) writes of a sense of catastrophe that links personality together. The very destruction of a unified self is its own kind of unity. In truth, there are catastrophic aspects to existence. Bion depicts a kind of Big Bang of personality, catastrophic explosiveness that sends bits and pieces of personality hurtling away from each other and their point of origin. What do we do with our catastrophic anxieties? Can depression keep up with them or is the latter, also, a kind of burnout?

We are not only catastrophic but have lots of pleasures, ecstasies, good moments, learning, work. But also catastrophic dreads that run through our bodies, soul, spirit. Our minds are populated by dreadful gods, good gods, a dreadful side of God, a good side of God. Good stuff, bad stuff – that's us!

Picture a baby discovering joy in being alive, a joy in having consciousness, joy of awareness. At the same time, at another level or another moment, dread can make you feel alive too. Freud wrote of the pervasiveness of anxiety. Winnicott described primal agonies. Bion touched on "nameless dread" that spreads through existence. Dread that links, unites, destroys, tears apart, inner war. M. Klein depicts anxiety and aggression tied to hunger and other states and functions. She calls the stomach a hell pit. Some anxieties Freud pointed to include separation, intrusion, depressive, castration, life and death. Nameless dread seems to take endless forms. Like a hero with a thousand faces (Campbell, 1949), there is no end to Satan.

A basic paradigm: baby goes into a state of anxiety. Mother tries to comfort the baby, soothe the anxiety to variable degrees and qualities of success. But things do not always go well. The baby may be colicky or feeling too much pain, perhaps there is some physical problem or irritation. If soothing does not work anxiety and discomfort can spiral until the baby goes into some kind of stupor, perhaps resembling aspects of catatonia. Self-numbing takes the place of soothing. All of us, to some degree, work with self-stimulating and self-numbing processes. We have a lot to learn to work with.

What happens when the baby's dread and anxiety meet the mother's dead spot rather than responsive soothing and caring? Or variable mixtures of responsiveness and absence, chronic states of being out of it, not there? In one case a mother came to see me when she found herself standing over her baby with a knife (Eigen, 1993). She could not bear the screaming, needs and demands for caring attention and help. She found herself withdrawing, going blank and deadened. She could not take being a mother and what it must involve. She pictured throwing her baby against a wall and terrified herself when she hovered over her baby girl with a knife. What happens to a baby in such a situation? Does her anxiety spiral and die out? Does she gasp for air and seek hyperstimulation? Does her capacity to pay attention become too frightening and diminish? Do we see chronic, attenuated versions of these moments in what we call bipolar, attention deficit, post-traumatic stress, depression, or in some cases surges of violence including mass murders by young people at work today? And all the therapeutic approaches, attempted waves of cure or amelioration, vogues and mental health reach-outs – workers trying to find moments that help.

If psychic distress is a persistent part of human life, so are attempts to work with and relieve it. Drilled holes in human skulls in prehistoric times were thought to be attempts to let bad spirits out. In some ways, what was called bad spirit might be related to what we might call bad attitudes or states. It has been noted that people in many cultures have gone crazy in two main ways, depression and schizophrenia, so-called emotional and mental dimensions or whatever you want to call them. Make up your own language and terms. They have been written about and portrayed from earliest times.

Arnie's glimpse of dead and dread expresses a real learning curve, emergence of more capacity to let these things in, let ourselves in, let psyche in. As if the psyche is knocking on the door. "Hello, is anyone home?" Are you home? Sometimes I'm home a little bit, tiny openings. Perhaps outright psychosis is a kind of breaking through the walls or seeping through veins and linings.

Deadness and aliveness come and go and mix in all sorts of ways. A few days ago I had a wonderful alive moment. After a two-and-a-half hour run, I felt amazing. During the run, fatigue and heart pains and lassitude were part of the brew. There were moments I felt I'd go home and just drop dead. So it was a surprise to feel marvelous all night long. I wonder if this is a kind of model for the baby coming through moments or periods of acute distress and opening to joy or bliss or peace. Even so, life does not stop throwing curve balls. That evening we went out to a restaurant with good friends but the woman we were with could not stop talking – yak, yak, yak. So I left her to my wife and I connected with her quiet, less talkative husband, both of whom had a genuine sensitive feel for life and welcome insights. And so it goes, as Kurt Vonnegut might write or Billy Joel sing of our many spectrums and their moments.

Dread and dead, let them in, don't let them in. If you can't open through psychoanalysis, try opening with Rumi. Have you read *The Guest House*? Say hello to yourself. Welcome guests of your being a little at a time, as much as you can take. Today, in this hour, if you are not feeling too good, if you are even more dead than usual, that's the way it is. A year or two from now you might feel more alive or even two minutes from now. No matter. That's just part of the wheel turning. So let it in.

Arnie let it in. "My God, maybe I didn't have such a perfect mother, maybe I didn't have such an idealized childhood. That doesn't mean good things didn't happen. If I speak to myself I can say, I did have good nourishing things happen in spite of it all. Because of it all. No need to split off, all good, all bad. It seemed all bad for a while. Then all good for a while. Hard to get a bigger view, take in the mix."

The psyche is crawling with bugs. The psyche is alive with beauty. I read somewhere when I was younger that creative people had extreme experiences in infancy. People disparaged that for a time but lately, it's making a comeback. Extreme highs, extreme lows. Maybe sometimes being even-keeled is a relief, maybe boring. Sometimes extremes come as a revelation: "O my God, there are different worlds!" Some creative people spend their lives writing about these worlds. Or painting or whatever use of self is given to them.

Participant: I wonder which comes first, sensitivity or extreme state. A chicken and egg situation?

Mike: Do you ever feel that way about yourself?

Participant: At times, yes.

Mike: More than at times?

Participant: Yes – more!

Mike: Which is first, chicken or egg?

Participant: It can go either way. Somehow I'm feeling sensitivity is primal, although it can be exacerbated by what it goes through.

Mike: We are sensitive babies too.

Participant: Yes. We are sensitive babies too.

Mike: Babies are very sensitive. They go from room to room, state to state. I know there is a range of states at birth. One baby comes out Apollonian, meditative, another like Ghenghis Khan. Since antiquity and likely before people have been documenting and trying to categorize or organize such varying temperaments and moods.

Arnie's beginning glimpse of primal realities dovetails with various psychoanalytic and trans-analytic visions. Bion feels we begin life with mixed states. And before birth, there were mixed womb states. Womb studies tell us that the womb is not simply a uniform environment. There may be some tendency toward homogeneity but it is also heterogeneous, sometimes better or worse. Sound can shock or soothe. There is some work that suggests embryos like Mozart. A lot goes on. Chemistry varies and even though there is no light in the womb some sense of light may exist. The womb guest can touch and close its eyes in certain ways and see phosphenes, a certain kind of light organically indigenous. Herman von Helmholtz studied and drew a series of phosphenes and Emmanuel Ghent honored this phenomenon by creating electronic music for a dance program called Phosphones. With eye pressure and other conditions, there is luminosity even in darkness.

Bion has a multiplicity of models touching varied tendencies and dimensions of psychic life. In one of his models, he feels at the beginning of life everything is animate. Everything is alive. In order to survive we need to de-animate enough to carry on and function. How do we de-animate, tone it down without losing total contact with this living well? Our brain and other organs have implicit inhibitory capacity as well as excitatory. The cerebral cortex, for example, inhibits and selects. On experiential levels, we have to learn how to work with excitatory-inhibitory tendencies.

I once questioned a teacher of mine, Father William Richardson [1993], a Jesuit priest, about aspects of our conundrums, like being caught between life and language. He wrote on Heidegger and later Lacan. Heidegger was into origins of language, origins of the pulse of life, relationships between Being and Truth. When he was a guest teacher at the New School he invited our small class to his apartment. I was talking about non-verbal dimensions of experience Heidegger expressed. Already a "contradiction" or "paradox" – talking about the non-verbal? And as was popular in the 1960s, feeling the feeling, the non-verbal truth of life. Feeling the thing itself. I think now of Steve Jobs dying and not having words for his experience, saying "Wow!" In class we were speaking, among other things, about how is it possible to speak, to express the unspeakable when no words would do? Father Richardson smiled gently, looked at me and said something like, "What are we supposed to do? Sit silently and say nothing, say "Ugh?" Father Richardson brought home in his Zen way the impossible in our everyday lives, moment-to-moment existence as impossibly possible. I think of the phrase in the morning prayers, "miracles of everyday."

The break or rupture between life and language is often emphasized but there is also continuity. Why are we so enthralled with living language? Find your favorite poet or psalms, whatever expressive form is alive for you. We speak of dead words or living words. When words are alive they don't diminish life feeling, they increase it. So there is not simply rupture between life and words. It depends, partly, how words are used and how life feels. In actuality, words can create life and bring dimensions of being into existence that were not there before the word was said in just that way.

Participant: A lifeline.

Mike: A lifeline. Words are funny – filled with all kinds of things – like lie in life. Is life a lie? How? In what ways? Or lifeline – a line of poetry can enliven and open life. Again a chicken and egg situation, life giving birth to words birthing life. When I read Rilke I feel worlds coming alive right before my very eyes, my very being, inside me. I'm watching him create the life I feel, new bits of life. We are explorers of ruptures between life and word and also their co-creation.

Freud emphasized tensions between discontinuity-continuity, including birth from womb to outside world – what a complex set of possibilities evoked by a sense of inside-outside. Bion, too, wrote there may be more continuity between in-womb and out-of-womb experience than is usually credited. Rupture-continuity is part of life, neither washes the other away but they can create all kinds of mixtures.

Participant: Words become a channel the stream rushes through as it discovers, "Yes!" it's just energy.

Mike: It opens wells, not just closes them.

Participant: It's a focusing of energy.

Mike: I used to call it a funnel but it's much more than that.

Participant: I was listening to a podcast about how when you learn the word for something it changes the way you think about it. In a way it literally creates a new way to live.

Mike: A new way, a new wave. It creates waves and ripples. Waves
and ripples have a nice feel, kind of post-field theory, but
also harking back to water images. Freud spoke of flooding
as a primal trauma. By that, he meant emotional, stimulus,
psychic, mental flooding. The idea that the psyche can be
flooded by its own existence may have pre-ancient roots.
Freud, too, admired Heraclitus' image of war between
elements as a basis for how the world works, destruction as
part of creation and vice versa. For Freud conflictual inner
organizations can be growth-producing and nourishing,
conflict and tension as part of the growth of co-nourishing
dimensions. It seems a patent observation that destruction is
part of existence. The music of the spheres on the one hand,
war between elements and structures on the other.

One of Bion's models is an inner war that has no end. Harold Bloom said
Shakespeare invented the human as we know it. In part, he was referring to
virtually unending inner and outer human conflict. Even in fantasy, what if
this, what if that? Bion felt that one of the functions of actual war in the
outside world was a kind of waking dream or nightmare in which we can
see projected what is in us and perhaps begin to catch on to aspects of our
makeup that we lack capacity to deal with. Can we grow capacity to work
with ourselves better, more fully?

Parallel with Bloom, I like to say Freud invented the psyche. Certainly,
this is not true. People have been talking, writing, drawing psyche a long
time. The word psyche itself is from Greek mythology. Freud picked up on
tensions between psychic structures with emphasis on creative-destructive
interactions. He liked to think he was creating a mythology of his own,
although acknowledged it drew on and partly reworked ancient images.
He remarked to Wilhelm Fliess that they were continuing the work of the
ancient mystery cults with emphasis on transformation.

If Freud "invented" the psyche, Jung expanded it and many psychoanalytic writers added to it. Bion furthered Freud and Jung's awareness of
how we deflect inner realities and often react outside to what is inside. Our
psychic awareness can be thin and fragile although we also have attention
that goes inward that with need and practice we can build upon.

Freud uses liquid and electrical images for psychic energy flow and being
stuck, evoking the charge and flow of living. For example, the term *cathexis*
is a kind of psychic charge that heightens particular areas of experience one
may project outward and react with little or no apparent awareness that it is
emanating, partly, from inner currents. So much inside us could be charged
and turned into heightened significance. Bion stresses observing such inner
happenings to the extent one can. So much of what is inside is deflected
outward. You deflect from self-awareness in important ways. I think of the

autistic child whose attention is caught by certain sensations or moves from one to the other in a kind of dance to keep pain away. So much to explore and use creatively if one begins catching on, so many rooms in the human house and potential division of labor. I like Bion's emphasis on what *can* you do, what are you good for? Or Casteneda's depiction of finding your place, your spot in the room, which Bion partly means by niche, a place where you can be productive, where you be you.

The power of deflection – we deflect from our feeling. Look at all the agonies a baby goes through. We don't want to do that all our lives. We'd rather have a war. We'd rather feel right and rage and blame someone. Look at all the pain out there, mutilated, liquefied bodies, all the weaponry to deflect. It's easier to create and fight a war because we don't have the equipment to see the weaponry inside, the mutilated, liquefied bodies inside, soul mutilations. We don't have equipment to see and work with all that has happened to us, all the negative, all the positive. It's easier to manufacture equipment to kill people than it is to find yourself. Look at the satisfaction some young people are getting murdering their peers, "mass murders" in schools, churches and stores. Revenge for – fill in the blank. Evening the score? Getting back at? Bion uses the term "evacuation" which is a little more than "projection," to evacuate, to get rid of pain, get rid of the psyche, get rid of what cannot be gotten rid of, another perverse meaning of finding yourself by losing yourself? In Kabbalah, we say what is inside is outside, what is outside is inside. This can work in keys of deep nourishment or obliteration.

Did you ever think of some commonality between delinquency and war? Winnicott noted that a function of acting out delinquency is to unconsciously (and perhaps semi-consciously in some way) call attention to the pain that is driving the criminality – pain that the delinquent does not have resources to deal with. It may be the human race has profound pain it cannot deal with and tries to call attention to in all kinds of ways. War is so horrific. Mutilation, beheading, fire, toxins, blood everywhere – it's as if we make the pain so great maybe we'll notice it – maybe someone will notice it. Do we have a diagnosis for war? We think we do it for external reasons and can point to violations that justify fighting. We think the cause is external while it mirrors and exacerbates internal pain we are at a loss in the face of. In war, we can beat an enemy, win or lose. But in relation to the internal pain with no name, we often seem relatively helpless or even self-destructive.

Participant: You mean like a psyche exploding?

Mike: That's often a piece of it. Fritz Perls (1992) spoke of implosion-explosion as phases in inner movement towards greater authenticity. The implosion or explosion may force you – often with help – to see something is there that needs attention and care. You have a chance of moving past the bombs towards getting the hang of feeling the feeling. Learning to get the feel of a state may create openings for what Perls calls existential authenticity. In a way, it's like taking your psychic temperature and working with the palette of life that is you. Interpersonally, dialogue or argument rather than war,

Participant: Melanie Klein said the psyche/self is at war, inner war.

Mike: Or as Bion, one of her analysands said, war without end. I also feel inner havens and so did she. One function of libido for Klein was to offset the bad feeling, life feeling offsetting a destructive force. Of course both are part of life. She wrote of an inner good object offsetting the bad. States have multiple functions. For example, an ideal sense can mitigate or exacerbate self-hate, depending on a host of factors. We are at the mercy of our psyche and our psyche is at the mercy of us. Let us hope, at least some of the time, compassion prevails and aids in benevolent self-transformation. The "good feeling" can be so much more than mercy (*chesed*) but if it can get to that it's come some way.

Participant: I was just reading in Bion passages about awareness of who and what you are just now listening to you and thinking about what I read I felt touched by the pleasure – I don't know what to call it – of being really aware of each minute of feelings, the pleasure of moments of feeling.

Mike: That is a precious capacity. So much of the time I am unaware of most of me, sometimes vacant or preoccupied or thoughtless. Often I identify with the simple child at the Seder, the one who asks, "What's going on?" Actually, that can turn into a useful attitude in sessions, just asking what's happening, what's going on here? What is this?

Participant: Staying with a feeling can be surprising. I have a relative who's been persecuting me for years. She keeps writing that she idealized me and I ignored her. Now she's after me, telling me horrible things about myself. After I received her last email I was enraged and had fantasies of revenge against her. I took pleasure in minute details of getting back at her. I talked to someone close to me about her who said, "You are her favorite scapegoat." And then he added, "You rejected her." His remark enabled me to begin to see myself from her point of view. I found myself praying for her and also praying she wouldn't bother me anymore. And then the amazing thing happened. My feelings turned into compassion. I was amazed after all this annoyance, irritation, hate – compassion.

Mike: Something opened.

Participant: A wall opened and now I'm feeling such compassion for her. I can't believe it.

Mike: Our feelings are amazing. Look at all the things, positive and negative, idealization, being ignored and pestered can lead to.

Participant: I was angry, felt compassion, and then the anger petered out. I'm really compassionate now.

Mike: Many do not realize this can happen. For example, if you get a rager in therapy he/she might feel justified raging all life long. But you work together twenty years and one may have experience where new dimensions of being open. Once it happens it's something like a conversion experience, a rebirth moment.

Participant: Like falling off the horse.

Mike: "My God, this exists."

Participant: I was thinking of Saint Paul falling off his horse on the way to Damascus, whether it was an actual or spiritual horse. We have a saying something like, "Get off your high horse," i.e., stop thinking you are superior, above things. I felt my persecutor was entitled to compassion as a human being, whether or not she deserved it.

Mike: Did you hear Obama sing "Amazing Grace?" Grace comes as a gift, an opening in life, in Being, whether we "wretches" deserve it or not. A gift that opens Life.

Participant: I keep thinking of the word "entitled, entitled.' In mythology people who feel entitled take, they just take and take.

Mike: It's such a mixed word. Entitlement can be part of the difficulty. At the same time, it can be a sense of appreciation that there is More. The pain of being hurt, deprived and entitlement go together. I'm thinking again of Winnicott's delinquent reacting, in part, to a sense of privation, a sense that something was taken away. In this case a sense of deprivation triggers entitlement, exacerbates it. One attitude that can emerge resembles a psychopathic sense that if I am going to get anything from life I have to get it myself – no one is going to give it to me, no one will or can help. At the same time there is a memory, however dim or intense, of some island of gratification, some kind of goodness that was lost. This lived psychology in people today recalls an ancient theory of the origin of evil as *privatio boni*, absence, privation, lack of the good. A lack or loss encoded in the biblical Genesis and Milton's *Paradise Lost*.

Participant: The woman's mother died when she was two. I wonder now if she was hoping I would give her what her mother couldn't and she was angry at my persistent failure.

Mike: While you were speaking of this woman who lost her mother, I remembered a person I worked with whose father died when he was four. He described his mother as hash and angry and his father as softer. As we spoke my patient felt at four he lost the softness in his life. He was experiencing a double hurt, loss of goodness and bombardment of abrasiveness, again something of a theme embedded in our spiritual mythologies. A good feeling lost or injured, even mutilated, and before you know it self-mutilation and hurting others becomes a kind of awful balance. One is at war with life and life is at war with oneself. We see today too many instances of injury redressed by murder, perhaps as a futile way to call attention to the pain of one's being. What does it take to build inner capacity to work with such pain?

The Bible is filled with relevant stories of loss and retribution. A loss of "paradise" is followed by sibling murder. One brother kills another over real or imaginary injury. Is this also a parable about different sides of our personality in ceaseless war? As injustice and crime pile up God decides to end the human race with a flood, then pulls back and merely destroys most of it and lets a handful survive to try again. It is no accident that emotional, psychic, stimulus flooding is one of Freud's primal traumas, feelings that are too much for one. Apparently God could not take the reality of his creation, real or imaginary, expressing the sensitive reactivity of our psyche in moments of rage and devastation, wedding creation-destruction. And yet something survives and tries again.

So many variations of such moments are part of our lives today. For example, the woman you were describing was hurt and became persecutory in the name of injustice done to her. You lucked out through therapeutic intervention of someone close to you opening larger, complex vision so you weren't tyrannized by smaller reactivity, at least for a time. Even with entry to more expanded consciousness, the smaller self comes back. You can count on it not vanishing.

Participant: I know.
[Laughter]

Mike: I'd like to try talking a little more about psychopathy and maybe contrast it a little with some aspects of schizophrenia because psychopathy seems to be having a resurgence and taking so many forms. You can find my little online book, *Age of Psychopathy* written during the Bush administration and Iraq war (http://www.psychoanalysis-and-therapy.com/ human_nature/eigen/pref.html). It's as if psychopathy is coming out of the closet in new ways but apparently has been part of human nature from time immemorial. I spoke about a feeling that seems part of a psychopathic attitude – if I'm going to get anything good out of life I've got to get it for myself any way I can. Freely given goodness by others seems missing or diminished in such an attitude. If goodness exists I've got to take it. Apparently goodness is perceived to be there and I feel justified to steal, lie, misrepresent, force, grab, seduce. In schizophrenia one may be more confused. The mother may represent herself as better than she is, e.g., all the hurt you feel isn't coming from me. I'm only doing good things for you. In contrast, the psychopath has a clear picture about the bad that is going on, clarity about a bad parent and feels justified in stealing what goodness one can. A schizophrenic orientation may wait for the good to appear. It may not be happening because something is wrong with him, something bad.

By contrast, the psychopath has a certain simple clarity: "I know the bad thing's happening and you're not going to talk me out of it. I'm going to get the good stuff in life and no one's going to stop me." Here a sense of entitlement rules. Psychopaths can develop a talent for manipulating psychotic confusion and anxiety to try to get what they think they want.

I'm thinking of a time in grammar school I stole a beautiful object another boy brought to class. When he realized it was missing he cried and cried and I brought it back. I was too conflicted to be a good psychopath or beatnik so became a psychotherapist.

[Laughter]

Dead and dread. Arnie has a dawning awareness of the depths of the negative in life. And the beginnings of more than a dawning awareness of how he deflects from negative and positive depths, deflects from himself. One of my favorite Paul Tillich quotes which I first heard some 60 years ago, something like, 'One is only as big as the amount of the diabolic in himself one can assimilate.' Diabolic, of course, usually refers to evil. It can also be part of the anabolic-diabolic duo, to build up and tear apart. Freud spoke of the death drive as a kind of falling apart and the life drive as building up, complements. Both take on many meanings and nuances in his work in different contexts. However we understand it, it's no small thing that Arnie begins to see his deflections. For so much of life, deflections are deflected, one looks away or, better, one does not, cannot see. Sometimes one sees imaginings one trics to deflect. In Arnie's case, there came a moment when he suddenly got interested in violence, world violence, inner violence. He began talking about violence everywhere. He spoke about his wife's violence and anger, especially when the children were young. He was the soft one, she was the angry one. Yet his own lapses were worse and he feels terrible about them. The things he did to the kids when they were young – how could he ever make up for them? Now he's thinking about all the bad things in life, inside and outside. Have you ever had a moment where you are just seized and start crying over what human beings have done to each other since the beginning of time. You see eternity, you see all time and all the ages marching by, and the tragedy of it, the tragic element. And you weep. And you weep. Included in your weeping is a sense of what was done to you and what you do to yourself. An instant of seeing. The next moment it may all be diverted again as the pain of the outside world pours in. Pain of the inside and outside worlds meet, all the bad outside, all the bad inside. Shifts happen back and forth. You see your makeup and want to be better, you see the makeup of the outside world and want to help if you can. You want to be a better person, trying to get more in touch with yourself and someone says, "What about the tragedies in Nigeria, Syria, Gaza?" Your efforts are deflected – the outside world is the problem just as you were beginning to get somewhere with the inside. Inner complaints, outer complaints deflect from the work at hand. You have to come to grips that if you are going to work with yourself it's not the same as saving the world. In Judaism there are thoughts like if you save one person, do one good deed you save the world. If you save yourself you save the world. quite a nice thought and project and spiritual moment. But you may have to get used to the reality that if you help yourself a little that is its own reward: you help yourself a little, and maybe a little more, a little better one moment, a little worse another. But an almost salvific sense grows when you feel the help, even a tiny bit, a tiny drop of help, self-help. It certainly may make life a tiny bit better for those around you – maybe. But what you do have is growing contact with yourself. "Hello, hello, anyone home?" And then the famous Biblical phrase *Hineni*– here I am. And all three words make a felt difference: Here I am. And they travel: "I'm here. What do *you* feel like?" "Oh, oh, my back is starting to hurt. But I'm here." Moments that happen big and little ways all through life, attention deflected inside-outside, back and forth. Deeper and deeper inside, more appreciative outside.

There may be something outside you really need to attend to. Or maybe something inside is calling you, "Hi, Michael. Come on in, I've been waiting for you." Freud pinned this double movement, turning against the self, turning against the other. But it can be a turn for the self and others as well. Energy turning inward, energy turning outward, good and bad depending on the context, both valuable, precious.

Here's one of many possible sequences. A few days ago I woke up on the dead side. I wasn't hurting anyone, not even myself. It's just the way the wheel turns. Little bits of grace peeked through and I started to come out of it and felt happier. When I went outside I saw neighbors had done what the city failed to do. They made pedestrian lanes on the road with chalk and paint and added a Stop sign as cars went too fast in our neighborhood.

Seeing the effort made to make our neighborhood better made me happy. There had been a spike in violence throughout the city including where we lived. More people seemed to be carrying guns in public.

When I drove my car to go shopping I happily observed the new lanes and caution. I quickly had a chance to test them out. A woman who wanted to cross the street was looking at me expecting me to speed up at the corner as was usually done. When I slowed down and signaled her to go ahead she just lit up. She couldn't believe I was letting her go. I could see for her it felt like a little bit of grace. On my way back it happened again at a bigger avenue. A man was running across the busy street and when he saw me coming he must have been afraid I would run him over because he stopped short. I made an arm gesture to signal it was OK waving him on. He looked surprised and happy and I felt happy. I didn't feel dead anymore, not that it's so awful feeling dead for a while. So many moments come and go including many bits of grace. A little baby gets moods that keep changing unless it gets stuck in one forever and ever.

After waking up on the dead side life gradually began to creep back in. Deadness wasn't deflected so much as part of an unfolding progression. Deflecting pain or other states seems more active-reactive, playing down, escaping unpleasant experiences or tendencies. Deflection has had survival value and has helped achieve positive outcomes. However, at the present time I'm not so sure the human race needs so much reactivity. With our immense world weaponry and near-instantaneous digital communication and amazing capacity for lies to become truth what we need is growth in our capacity to process ourselves, our psychic beings, work with ourselves in better ways.

In Freud's gymnasium, there was already tension between autonomic reactivity, old brain emotionality and a cortical need to select, inhibit, find ways of steering through and between outbreaks. What is it we see when we look in our psychic mirrors? What is it we can do, sustain, tolerate, work with? Growing inner equipment to work with ourselves seems a Number One priority, if or insofar as we can do it.

Sometimes need to develop equipment for life manifests in strange ways. A neighbor stops in front of a pharmacy and sees a man pull out a gun. It looks like he is demanding money from another man who proceeds to pull out his gun. There they are on a busy street facing each other with their guns. My neighbor is so disgusted and appalled he simply drives away without even reporting what he is seeing to the police. Is it that violence has reached a point where one is more disgusted than appalled? I read a report that an armed man tried to break into an FBI outpost and a standoff ensued for hours. Right-wing strategists have been encouraging violence as a means of cleansing the body politic, offering the American Revolution as a "model."

Our powerful weaponry is part of our greater technology that is part of our creativity and lethal skill. We are poisoning the environment as well as injuring ourselves. If we can develop a psyche less lethal to itself, we may have a better chance of helping the environment and each other. Look at the fights between different schools of psychoanalysis and varied therapeutic approaches. I would like to think the mental help field is becoming more open and mutually respectful, learning how to use our varied viewpoints and forms of co-nourishment better. Attempts to utilize and integrate findings of warring schools is an important attitude. If such an attitude could become more a part of the dominant worldwide culture we might be able to get a little closer to what Levinas (1969) describes as proximity with difference, a sense that we are all near however far.

We have equipment to do terrible things to each other and equipment to heal, care and help. Both may be growing at an accelerating pace. To speak metaphorically, we may be able to kill more people in half an hour than in the whole First World War. We are better at being lethal and can only hope that benevolent realism keeps pace. We have a psychical life filled with dramas, problems and difficulties we don't know how to work with. To what extent can learning grow? To what extent can psyche and psychoanalysis say hello to each other, greet and give? Jesus said or prayed, "Forgive them, they don't know what they're doing." Can we forgive each other, forgive ourselves, develop awareness of our makeup in ways that mend and open in spite of ourselves? Little by little life creeps in. How much life can we stand? Lord, send us little bits of grace we can digest that can work with us.

One of the things I loved about Alfred Adler was his emphasis on brotherly love. It was not something I was used to in psychoanalysis but very much part of lived existence. Adler dared to say it and in his way, so did Freud. What else did Freud do but show many ways love works? Adler underlined a tension between love and power. One might say freeing love and love of power, although, in a deep sense, love is a power too. The power of love is a common phrase but is work it can do so common? Many authors describe ways capacities feed each other, complexities of nourishment and strife. Some say we can make our brains evolve (Strauss, 1966). Harsher and better environments affect our brains, why not our attitudes and emotions? We have better and worse inner environments. You need to find your own way to work with your brain, to work with yourself. So many ways to work with your psyche have grown through the centuries, prayer, music, athletics, psychoanalysis, add your own. Different schools have their formulas, ways of adding and collapsing in on themselves.

We are rightly worried about atom bombs. Who's going to do what when? But even that can be a deflection outward. A big question is what are you going to do with the atom bomb in you, the atom bomb that *is* you. We are our own atom bombs as well as the psychic bombs couples and groups produce. What can little tastes of goodness do in the face of the atom bombs we are? We have plenty to work with but little tastes can go a long way.

References

Balint, M. (1956). *Primary Love and Psychoanalytic Technique*. London: Routledge.

Bion, W. R. (1970). *Attention and Interpretation*. London: Routledge.

Bloch, D. (1977). *So the Witch Won't Eat Me: Fantasy and the Child's Fear of Infanticide*. Lanham, MD: Jason Aronson.

Campbell, J. (1949). *Hero With a Thousand Faces*. San Francisco. New World Library.

Eigen, M. (1993). *The Electrified Tightrope*. Ed. A. Phillips. London: Routledge

Eigen, M. (2015). *Feeling Matters*. London: Routledge.

Levinas, E. (1969). *Totality and Infinity*. Pittsburgh: Duquesne University Press.

Perls, F. S. (1992). *Gestalt Therapy Verbatim*. Ed. M. V. Miller. Gestalt Journal Press.

Richardson, W. R. (1993). *Heidegger: Through Phenomenology to Thought*. New York: Fordham University Press.

Straus, E. (1966). *Phenomenological Psychology: The Selected Papers of Erwin W. Straus*. New York: Basic Books.

Chapter 2

Bits of Bion and Multiple Undercurrents

Very few people address my inner concerns the way Bion did. By that, you may think that I'm confessing inner deformity or even madness, two of Bion's basic interests.

I'm not saying he covers everything I feel or am but he does touch areas in ways few others have, at least for me, and that has been a difference.

Not only did he give imaginative expression to difficult areas of lived experience, but he seemed to pursue his vocation even more freely after being rejected by colleagues. I wonder if he relished difficulties rather than be "drowned by honors and sink without a trace." He was pretty well accepted by the London Kleinian community until the 1960s, after Melanie Klein's death, and the flowering of works that were sometimes thought mystical or idiosyncratic (Eigen, 1998). Some accused them of signs of dementia or senility. Referral sources dried up and he accepted an invitation to work in Los Angeles in 1968.

Trouble continued as the Los Angeles Psychoanalytic Society did not accept him as a member. One of the ironies of an often conflicted or even warring psychoanalytic field – a former President of the British Psychoanalytic Society rejected by the Los Angeles Society. In contrast to Kleinians in London who felt he was no longer Kleinian enough, the Los Angeles Society felt he was too Kleinian. He shared what was inside him with the world, and apparently, it was it blew fuses.

Nevertheless, workers like Donald Meltzer stood by him, and as a demonstrative gesture, Meltzer left the British Society. It was during this later period that references to the dangers of working without a license or official support appeared in Bion's work. He wrote of phases of therapy in which a schizophrenic patient might seem to be getting worse before getting better and the therapist's anxieties of lawsuits from the patient's family. Nevertheless, in Los Angeles, enough colleagues supported him and went into analysis and/or supervision with him so that he was able to make a living and continue his creative work, which kept blossoming till he passed away in 1979, at 81 years old.

DOI: 10.4324/9781032658926-3

At the end of *A Memoir of the Future* (1991), he expresses his wish to have written this dream-fiction-truth memoir without memory, desire, common sense, understanding. He hoped it would come from and meet him and us from an open place, a gesture of the creative unknown. But he, alas, accepts inevitable failure and wishes us a "Happy Lunacy and a Relativistic Fission." You will find three dots ... near the beginning of the Introduction and three dots ... at the start of the Epilogue suggesting there is more before and after. More to come and all kinds of madness and explosiveness parts of a larger process. Are we in the middle of eternal incompletion and can never say all there is to say or can be said? I'm tempted to try to write my own little formula something like: ... experiencing ... Instead of "That's all folks" at the end of a Bugs Bunny cartoon, "To be continued ..."

Bion observed and urged complexity and multiplicity. Every emotion is made up of infinite infinities. That doesn't stop oversimplification and wars continue, Me vs. You. Wars are often oversimplifications of complex problems. Boundaries and supplies (e.g., food) are two of the "simple" primitive reasons for war, although Homer pictures an erotic theft as a cause or excuse for epic war. Egos (e.g., vanity and power) complicate physical or emotional needs and things can get violent fast. Me vs. You can apply between individuals, groups, nations. It often applies within one's own self – Me vs. You bits, elements or systems within a person. Who's right, who's wrong, top dog – bottom dog, it goes on and on everywhere in various forms. Sustaining a partnership model – we're in this together – seems to present enormous difficulties. Winnicott (1986, pp. 228-259) alluded to this when he remarked that democracy is a very small part of the psyche. Much development lies ahead and is needed or the pseudo-simplification and damage of war will continue.

One can argue there is much to be gained by war: all-out use of self and resources, release and experience of vital aggression, mutual fertilization of cultures, to name a few. I remember reports of neuroses cured by being able to kill without guilt. However, there were many psychological casualties. Bion's (1948) work with groups focused on war trauma. Emotional and physical violence in response to difficulties and threat seem to be part of the way we are made, part of the life form we are. So is problem solving, care, love, friendship and something so needed in political life as well, tolerance of ambiguity.

Our life form presents many challenges. If we evolve past a certain point integrity can become as and sometimes more important than survival. How we survive, psychic quality grows in importance as new dimensions of experience open. What it feels like to be a human being, quality of aliveness takes on more value. Some pieces of my life may begin to say, I don't want to be this or that kind of human being. I'd like to be a better person, a more human human. I don't know if I can be any different. I'll never stop hurting people and people will never stop hurting me. But that's not all we are. There are moments we are blessings for each other. We wonder if and how we can try to try to be a little better. I think of Samuel Beckett's "Fail again, fail better." We give up giving up and go back to work, a little more open, caring. Fritz Perls used to say take little vacations from yourself throughout the day. Giving up, letting go, oscillates with perseverance. Giving up for a time can let systems reset or make room for something new to appear.

Bion's advice to the analyst to be without understanding, memory and desire opens space for the unknown. I think of Heidegger's clearing in which truth (*aletheia*) appears unconcealed, in the present context perhaps a bit of psychic reality. Bion used the notation F in O to depict the psychoanalytic attitude, faith in unknown or unknowable reality. Faith has an open attitude in therapy sessions making it more possible for unknown emotional realities to register and appear. Milner (1987) liked writing Bion's O as 0 (zero), linking with Buddhist emptiness, *sunyata*. I like linking it, too, with *tohu habohu*, the chaos-nothingness in *Genesis* that God trembles over in the moment of Creation.

In one of my meetings with Bion, he said, "I use the Kabbalah as a framework for psychoanalysis." We spoke about the *Zohar* and other topics. In Kabbalah, *Ein Sof* stands for the nameless, infinite God of creation and "prior to" creation. Other names were also given to a sense of an infinite nameless creative essence/process, e.g., *Atzmus* which I can't help partly associating with *Atman*. Remember, Bion had a Hindu nanny his first eight years as a little boy in India. I often associate O with what I call the creative unknown, whether within a soul, person, or world.

Bion's O draws from many backgrounds. In *Two Papers; The Grid and Caesura* 1989) Bion has more quotes from Saint John's "dark night of the senses" than he does Freud. He relates Saint John's expressions of the mystical journey to his own depiction of the psychoanalytic attitude, being without memory, expectation, understanding and desire. Sometimes I like depicting his F in O as a kind of Openness to O.

When he lists capacities and attitudes that imprisoned him he calls understanding "the greatest Bug-bear of all." We assume it is good to be recognized and understood yet understanding can be a trap, a prison in its own way too. Does understanding keep opening or does it close the door and turn into a belief system? We see the fight and punishing wars between belief systems all too rampant in our world today. It can be an awful thing not to be understood. Miss-understanding is common. Yet at times tension or conflict between understandings and points of view can be reduced to one of us is wrong, me vs. you.

I think of Emmanuel Ghent saying he felt seen only once in his life. It was a momentary touching of eyes with the Dalai Lama at a seminar by the latter in Los Angeles. Mannie must have been in his late sixties or early seventies. A look, a moment, an instant – seen, recognized, understood the only time in his life in one instant, never before or after. A reference point moment that defines something about the human spirit and makes me wonder if the soul can be a bit like a betta fish, a little goes a long way. Mannie and I were friends and he told me this at dinner, but if you don't know his work, here's a good taste (Ghent, 1990). Mannie was a wonderful pianist, composer and before psychiatry, an amazing software engineer at Bell Labs.

Bion understood that "understanding" a schizophrenic part of the self can feel confining, imprisoning, distorting. In a later collection (Bion, 1984) of papers he showed how some of his "interpretations" of dreams could open and others close the movement of dream-work. Understanding can be awful or awesome depending on how it functions in a given moment. There's a part of us that does not want to be pinned down, can't bear being pinned. And there's a profound sense in which nothing can pin it down. There is something in us unknown, a mystery, at times horrifying, at times glorious, everything between yet also beyond anything one can name or think. Beyond anything we know or can know about ourselves, a sense of unknown Presence (some might say Absence). Saying this is not against knowledge or understanding, which may be inexhaustible, but acknowledging more or other is part of our being too.

Participant: I'm thinking of the polarity between the individual and collective, my sense of self moving between what I might call China and America. As an American I push the individual but need the collective. I picture two fish swimming together, almost a kind of yin-yang but Japanese. How does one reconcile the individual and collective? The self needs some kind of grounding acknowledgment, a culture, a family, a group. The self needs *us*.

Mike: A perennial and important issue with different thoughts and models through the ages. We wouldn't be here if we weren't born into a family. If the family put us out into the woods with the wolves we probably wouldn't survive. So we stay with the wolves in our family.

Participant: Yes.

Mike: Your use of China-United States for collective-individual together with a Japanese yin-yang is colorful and pertinent. Tensions and conflicts between individual-collective are rabid in the world today. How to work towards co-nourishment of capacities and tendencies rather than war is a basic challenge. Martin Buber's contrast of collective and communal (co-union) is aspirational but real nonetheless (Elkin, 1972). Reaching for more supportive relationships between each other and our capacities has a long way to go. To what extent can we, will we grow into this needed work? Our sense of self and being is precious but is also deeply dependent on atmospheric conditions of the day. I'm thinking of the Cain and Abel story and the transformation Cain underwent to become a builder of cities for all the Abels (and many Cains) to live and use their capacities. Again, paradoxical yin-yang moments.

Participant: The self comes forth too. How does that happen? Bion seemed to become Bion because the group wasn't that important to him.

Mike: In an important way, yes. On the other hand Winnicott would not have been Winnicott and Bion would not have been Bion without their passage through Melanie Klein. They were very much themselves as they kept going but without significant mediums of passage it is hard to see how that could have happened. Had the world of psychoanalysis not existed they could not have made the kind of contributions they did. Other contributions in other contexts perhaps, even likely. But they furthered birth of the world that gave birth to them.

I'm thinking of Erroll Garner as an example of idiosyncratic relations between individual–collective, maybe a little like your example of Bion and the group. Erroll Garner was quite a jazz pianist with colorful, sustaining chords and rhythm. When as a child he began to play spontaneously his mother got him and his sister a music teacher to help further their skills. His sister was a good student, learned to read music and play well. Erroll, however, didn't, couldn't or wouldn't learn to read music and continued playing by ear. If he heard his teacher or sister play a work he would try to fool his teacher by making believe he was reading the score but playing by ear. His teacher finally fired him and continued with his sister. As he grew and began to enter the jazz world his gift of being able to play almost anything by ear served him well. When he was interviewed later in life and asked, "How do you do it?" He replied, "How do you get horny?"

In the 1960s we used to say, "Do your thing." So many people doing their own thing. Differences stimulate and add to creativity. Zen said something like this, too – find where you are and practice. Freud talked about repetition compulsion and he was not wrong. Yet no two "repetitions" are identical. Bateson used the term "news of difference" What is different about this "repetition?" When I was a kid I heard sayings like "No two snowflakes are alike." When I was a little older, "You can't step into the same river twice." A little later still I wondered – "Can you step into it once?" There are moments you feel it, "Ah, the river!" And some of those moments are decisive.

I suspect my first contact with D. T. Suzuki was his *Introduction to Zen Buddhism* with an introduction by Jung. My contact and exploration grew and deepened over the years. In autobiographical writings, he spoke of starting going to a Zen temple after his father died. He would go home early mornings to see his mother gardening then return to the *sangha* to sit. He was assigned koans to work with like *mu* but failed to achieve enlightenment. At some point, the Zen master he practiced with suggested he go to Chicago where he could have a job translating Buddhist writings into English, at which he was adept. I believe the first Sutra he translated was the *Lankavatara Sutra,* which is free online and is my favorite. While he was translating sutras he came across the sentence, "The elbow doesn't bend backward," which triggered an Enlightenment experience. None of his teachers thought of giving him that one to meditate on. The path is not straight, one does not know what will lead to what. He could not have pictured this would happen in Chicago while translating a sutra into English. Yet the experience was definitive, leaving him with a sense that no one can tell you whether this is real or not, not your teacher or anyone else. You are the sole witness, experiencer and verifier, an N of 1.

Participant: He had to find it himself.

Mike: He found it himself when he was doing something else, something material to help disseminate Buddhism in the U.S. Something material – writing for publication. Yet thought-feeling-sensing were essential and the unexpected happened. A kind of implosion or explosion – a realization, more than aha – a life-changing moment, an Opening. There are moments that change us, shift gears, open self. He was absorbed in a task that opened a world, perhaps you might call it an insight into being. He did it, had to do it himself but without the task, the background of knowledge and immersion in Zen culture could it have happened? The prefix co- in Buber's (Elkin, 1972) communion (co-union) implies an important degree of togetherness or as mystics sometimes say, I-yet-not-I. There are important ways that separation-union go together. I've sometimes tried to write this as a distinction-union structure that characterizes or is part of our experiential being.

I'm thinking, too, of Jesus saying, "When two people gather in my name I will be there." Perhaps not just I will be there but I *am here.* Akin to Jacob saying after a night wrestling with an Angel, "You were here and I didn't know:" Or, better, "You *are here.*" It's not just singular identity, it's not an anonymous collectivity. It's more a personal communal sense in addition to the individual and collective, at once both and neither.

  The enlightenment or wisdom literature is filled with paradox. Solomon tells us there is nothing new under the sun. Rebbe Menachem Schneerson tells us God creates the world anew from nothing each moment. Nothing is replicable. Everything is new. Yet we may find ourselves moaning about the same old thing – another war or doldrum. I think of a German "proverb" my analyst told me: "Man thinks straight, God thinks crooked; God is smart, man is stupid."

There is something to be gained by understanding Bion's remark, "I feel imprisoned by understanding." On the one hand, thank God for understanding – it's freeing. Yet I can feel imprisoned by it and the kinds of freedom it offers. A patient may feel misunderstood by our understanding because it is *our* understanding, our particular way of seeing, a particular viewpoint that he may feel misses the mark. We are limited by our understanding and the ways we understand. Too often belief or even delusion may be part of it. A patient may say, "You feel you understand me but I feel pinned down by it. Your understanding is engulfing, suffocating. It doesn't let me be me – it doesn't let me breathe."

I so appreciate cognition and deep levels of understanding. They are part of the life form we are. As are reason, common sense, memory, desire. Kafka said, "I am a memory come alive." "My life is an incomplete moment." So many have written so well on these capacities, functions, states and more.

Yet we also feel imprisoned by the life form we are. There is an ache for something more, past our limits. Over and over Saint Augustine reaches a place of knowledge and understanding and then expresses a need to go beyond them. For mystics, understanding is not enough. Saint Paul wrote of a peace that passes understanding. Some spoke of union with God. States of open wonder can fill one with the beauty of nature. Or from the Psalms, "My cup runneth over." There are many ways of sensing and undergoing such moments.

Fritz Perls used to speak about implosions-explosions and deeper authenticity. One might also speak of inbursts-outbursts opening something further. One can suddenly burst into or out of oneself as part of our unexpected journeys.

There is much to gain meditating on what Bion may mean by calling functions that enrich us – reason, common sense, understanding – prisons. Too often we confuse our "take" on reality with reality itself and get rudely thrown around by the unexpected, unanticipated, un-symbolized real. Socrates long ago pointed out how belief systems are taken as truth, something as prevalent and vicious now as then. What we call understanding Bion calls the "greatest Bug Bear of all." Socrates was put to death for his endeavors, while Bion, whatever his struggles, left England for Los Angeles for the last decade of his life.

For more on the destructive capability of "false knowledge" you might read my essay on omniscience (Eigen, 1993). Too often in the public body bits of real knowledge can be used as lies to achieve power or gain. During the Cold War, I was afraid someone would press the button because they thought they knew something. At the moment, nuclear threat is again used as a weapon in a war for position and territory.

Participant: Are you scared now too?

Mike: Not in the same way yet. For Trump [the President of the U.S.A. when this seminar took place] it appears to be a power game. He'll try to one-up the other on power. It's blatant, not subtle at all. There is a limit to power, one can only go so far before getting knocked out by someone with more power. You can't keep on asserting power without someone asserting more power. But during the Cold War there were many subtleties and nuances.

Omniscience is more subtle than omnipotence. Thinking you know something other people don't is much worse. You may press the button thinking you know something about what the other is going to do. You may press the button for an imagined rather than real threat. That's different from pressing the button just to show them, one-up them. The bully on the playground gets knocked out by a bigger bully but the know-it-all finds ways of winning in more subtle ways that can be far scarier in the long run. During the Cold War the two parties managed not to do that. They possessed some degree of what Piaget called "decentering" so that they managed to see the situation from enough angles to avoid the button. Piaget writes of shifts from an egocentric attitude to an ability to decenter to entertain a multiplicity of perspectives. Enough "decentering" went on between leaders of the Cold War to avoid the fatal moment. Nevertheless, it is possible, at some point, that a know-it-all outsmarting himself will heighten catastrophic possibilities.

Participant: I'd like to translate the 'mental prison' idea into something I can use. I wrote down 'understanding requires a standpoint' – so that's why it's imprisoning, because it fixes you in time and place. It stops you from being in a moving present. But then this notion of omniscience and decentering is actually another form of fixity, it's a negation of time and place. That's why it's more terrifying than the Trump you know, a person who's actually right in the present. It's a different form of understanding, one that really stops time.

Mike: Did you write about this?

Participant: I just wrote this.

Mike: I mean, are you going to write about this?

Participant: Hurry up, publish it now!

Participant: I'm not like you. I don't write a book a year.

Laughter

Mike:	Every six months. Make an op-ed for the *Times* or *Huffington Post*.
Participant:	Tomorrow, Peter, tomorrow.
Participant:	But I do think that's the thing about understanding, that is why it's imprisoning.
Participant:	Can you say more about omniscience and negation?
Participant:	Omniscience is the pure negation of time.
Mike:	That's what they say about God.
Participant:	How does it negate time?
Participant:	It negates temporality.
Participant:	The present?
Participant:	It's a negation of the present, that's what makes it so terrifying.
Mike:	God rules everything, there's no temporality, it's atemporal, eternal.
Participant:	No movement.
Participant:	It's the end of a present. the beautiful thing about the present is it's-
Mike:	Three dots ...
Participant:	The three dots ... exactly ...
Mike:	In a way, Bion talks about being imprisoned by everything that helped him. I love his early work but there may also be a way he felt imprisoned by it. He moved from emphasis on K and –K to F in his later work, from knowledge and understanding to faith, which he partly defined as an open attitude of being without understanding, reason, memory, common sense or desire. I've sometimes liked expressing it as "creative unknowing." He wrote about K and –K, L and –L, H and –H, knowledge, love, hate and their negative counterparts, internal attacks on knowledge, love, hate, attacks on linking. In a way, attacking linking is also a kind of link, an anti-link, a catastrophic link, the link of no-link. I'm thinking of my childhood and how his depiction apes some experiences of building and tearing apart in play, mixtures of creation-destruction that form life. Bion never added a minus before his F notation. He described the latter as the psychoanalytic attitude, a kind of avenue of access to unknown/unknowable emotional reality.

Is faith in the creative process at the bottom of all one writes? Bion admits that he failed in writing through faith alone. All the cognitive-emotional functions that make up and beset the human condition crept into his work – he could not have written without them. And yet the deep unknown is part of it. A destructive force in life brought him closer to an even deeper force for which there is no name. He tried the notation F in O, openness to the forever unknown. A deep sense in life that perhaps informs the five, six, seven or eight senses we like to name.

There are literary movements or gestures that try to strip language of its structure and meaning, attempts to get at or create raw experience in itself. *Finnegan's Wake* is one such attempt. Or to add even more humor (human) Erica Jong's "zipless fuck" in *Fear of Flying*. What kind of flying you might ask! Another "f" word. Bion says he would like to write, "abandon hope all ye who expect to find any facts" in this work whether scientific, aesthetic or religious – zipless writing, zipless sessions – but his efforts were doomed. I'm thinking now of wars in psychology between evidence, theory, love and the work of the living psyche. A living psyche that seems to stress and sometimes blow apart the disciplines that seek to study or tame it. We think of Keats's depiction of the poet living in ambiguities and mystery without irritably reaching after facts or reasons, a position he called "negative capability" in an 1817 letter to his brothers. Here "negative" is a very positive capacity. Bion would also quote Saint John of the Cross's dark night of the senses and soul as opening deeper access. Is Bion phobic about being trapped in his own makeup he enjoys using, a psychophysical organism that at the same time houses an Opening That Has No Name? People with such phobias can be extremely prolific.

As so many writers know, in some ways all writing is a necessary failure. A Voice told me years ago to stop trying to get the thing itself and settle for what is possible, what you *can* do. And lo, between the cracks Waldo appears. Spirit peeks through. You can't make it come but it comes of itself. If you have to write, called to write, a kind of inside writing force that's an invitation as well as pressure, it pays off in a way hard to describe (ah words), not necessarily a best seller or Pulitzer prize or lots of money but it pays off in a real sense.

Some of you may know Bion was embarrassed to get a medal for bravery in World War 1, when he was a tank commander in his late teens. He would hardly depict his state as brave so much fear went into it. Later he became president of the British Psychoanalytic Society and felt something similar. He ironically remarked about being loaded with honors and sinking without a trace. As mentioned above, that was nothing he had to worry about. As his work unfolded it aroused enough criticism and rejection for him to move from London to the Wild West in America.

Silence-speech. We are both. Thinking of a New School Heidegger class with Father Richardson, a Jesuit priest, at his apartment. Moved by Heidegger's depiction of truth (aleithea) appearing in a clearing of Being I spoke about the richness and importance of non-verbal aspects of experience and Father Richardson replied, "What are we going to do this afternoon, sit here and say ummm?" I immediately felt in his remark and tone profound appreciation of the non-verbal but here we were, a graduate Heidegger class.

So we will speak and it's imperfect. Imperfect communication – is there any other kind? We make allowances for each other and oneself, reset, renew, try again, come closer-farther, and the dialogical work continues.

If you are going to be with another human being, whether a patient, child, colleague, partner, friend, student, you have to assume a mixture of understanding and not understanding as part of the structure. And it is not so unusual for the unknown area of not-understanding to be closer to the truth or be a potential vehicle of truth, than understanding, which too often is prejudiced or even tyrannical and self-righteous. One might say, "I'm not sure I understand what you are trying to tell me. Can you say more?" Usually, there is room for more.

This doesn't mean there is no understanding but that what understanding happens is incomplete and subject to misunderstanding. You likely are often with someone where something is understood, felt, sensed, some commonality on some personal level in some way. There might be a sensed connection that is meaningful but not verbalizable. Still, you must assume not understanding or even no understanding as part of the structure of the situation. You also have to assume an area of aloneness, not being there as well as being there for each other and oneself. Too often people get angry at the non-communication or miscommunication, or not being there and don't get, don't appreciate or miss the little moment someone sees you or you see yourself. I've heard people describe one moment in their lifetime that made a difference, one moment of being seen and seeing. The one tiny big moment that comes and goes and gives a sense, this is real, life is real, you are real.

Participant: That's an anchor that allows you to have all the …

Mike: It becomes a frame of reference, even at times the reference point for everything. William Blake writes of a moment in each day Satan cannot find, a moment that reframes the feel and meaning and life of the day. Near the end of one of his last books, *A Memoir of the Future* (1991, p. 578) Bion writes about reason, common sense, understanding, being understood, memories, desire, and the like, "All these will, I fear, be seen to have left their traces, vestiges, ghosts, hidden within these words, even sanity, like 'cheerfulness', will creep in." This is a very different way of writing than the way he wrote his early papers, which he said were meant to get referrals. I love his early as well as later work, but something kept opening, and opening some more. The "failure" he was "doomed" to was tolerating and even accepting what's missing or wrong in the writing in order to let what's in the writing shine – good advice for authors and a partial model for other areas of life.

I've written about "sanitized sanity" in several places; for example, *Toxic Nourishment* (1999), the chapter, "Soundproof sanity and fear of madness." Winnicott's relation to madness grew as he aged, increasingly valuing creative madness, distinguishing it from destructive madness. Fear of the latter inhibited the former, but as he grew, his relationship to creativity kept developing.

Linking "cheerfulness" with "sanitized sanity" reminds when being a child and telling someone your deepest pain and they (the adult), "Don't worry, perk up, it'll be OK." Well, it hasn't been OK, all the hells of life and childhood agonies, but grown-ups told me things like that since I was a little boy. Cheerfulness? Well, "cheers," may have special meaning in Great Britain, like l'chaim, or skoll, or nostrovia and, after all, alchohol is called "spirits," and spirit is associated with mood, feeling, attitude as well as special life dimensions.

Good feeling-bad feeling; bad feeling-good feeling, back and forth, a kind of rhythm of existence (Eigen, 2004). It's not always bad to be cajoled away from a dark moment but just as Bion felt ashamed of his medal for bravery, or ironically feared the honor of being President of a psychoanalytic institute would lead to being sunk without a trace, so he feared his writing might become acceptable, respectable and unread. He seemed to associate "success" with a certain kind of human failure. What if Satan had not incurred God's wrath, where would creativity be now? And the flow of life, beautiful, crazy, sweet, ironic, funny, horrifying, inspiring, crushing, uplifting. A palette that does not stop adding colors, moments.

Bion asks why write then if you may be unread. One might ask, why fight (war), why do psychoanalysis (work)? Before getting to Bion's response to the question he asks about writing, here are a few pulses of my own. Writing redeems you. Writing redeems something in life, it lets spirit and the spark of life speak. It lets demons speak. Isn't that linked with the Greek Daimon, the voice Socrates listened to? The Muse of the poets? God's voice in the Bible? Emerson's "genius"?

And what else can being unread mean? For one thing, it means not being able to read oneself, to read one's soul, one's inner being. What an awful thing, to be illiterate when it comes to soul reading. We speak of the Book of Life, life's writing. Isn't that part of what we try to do when we write – read life, read life's writing, let life speak, let life write. And yet we also unread ourselves, perhaps to clear space, redress a wrong, seek another fresh start or, simply, try to become less saturated. Reading-unreading, we go our way. The moving beat of time in the "Rubaiyat" of Omar Khayyam can't help but have a simpatico Shakespearean ring. One gets a feel of birthing processes that do not stop.

Freud spoke of death anxiety being part of birth. There are ways, too, one might speak of birth anxiety being part of death. Winnicott pictures fear of beginnings, if severe, hits as the personality began to form. Aspects of dying out of personality can be part of fear of beginnings. Psychic death became a prominent theme in literature in the wake of horrifying wars. Analogous dying out in face of trauma can be part of individual experience as well.

How does one read oneself? How does one read one's personality? How is a deep self within writing you? It can be an awful thing to fall into the hands of the living psyche and an awful thing not to.

In *Attention and Interpretation* (1970) Bion writes about a tension between what he calls Genius/Messiah and Establishment, a "binary" that has been part of culture since antiquity and before. Bergson's tension between conservative and intuitive tendencies in creative processes is a kind of dialectical relation or what Winnicott might call paradoxical interweaving of new-old, spontaneity-tradition, permeating-opposing tendencies. William Blake called Satan the true hero of Milton's *Paradise Lost,* one of Bion's favorite poems. Blake called Satan energy and energy divine delight. For Bion, Genius/Messiah could be an oppositional movement or new idea breaking walls of the Establishment, forcing new organization and growth. One sees variations of this in schools emphasizing reason and/or inspiration. Oh, you mischievous little devil is a phrase I heard throughout childhood. Of course, devil has evil in it and the phrase "evil, be thou my good" has many implications. Recently, in an online group, Stewart Morton suggested that God-Satan is the Establishment and Christ the Mystic, the birth of the new, that which is not pinned down, ever renewing Life.

Bion (1990) also wrote about catastrophe as a link. The very falling apart of personality can act as a link that defines identity and in some way holds a person together. Dispersal as link, a paradoxical dialectic between bits and pieces and reorganizing that can take many turns, destructive and creative. Law, rebel, revolutionary, hate, compassion and birth that never stops. Can one make room for the psyche in one's life? Can one tolerate and learn to support the growth of psychic being? To what extent and in what ways can one partner one's own life processes?

Let me get back to Bion's question, "Why write then ... ?" Let me tell you why as it comes to me now: because it redeems you. It redeems something in life, it lets the spirit speak. It lets the Holy Spirit speak, lets the spark of life speak, it lets the demons speak, the creative Daemon, Emerson's "genius." Bion uses this Emersonian term in *Attention and Interpretation* (1970) where he writes about a genius or messiah aspect of personality, creative spirit evoking new life, life as new. A thread in human history akin to Bergson's intuition (a term Bion also uses) or mystic expression of the newness of being. Bion quotes a variety of poets, scientists, writers who, however miserable their lives, attest to a creative dimension. For William Blake a moment that lights existence. Marion Milner wrote of the most significant moments in her day which often were little pockets of Eternity.

Bion, unable to resist the call of ironic wisdom, wrote of the danger of one's work becoming "acceptable, respectable, honored and unread."

Why write then? "To prevent someone who KNOWS from filling the empty space." (his capital letters, 1991, p, 578). The filled space which is always empty, room for more, room for life's spark.

I'm thinking, too, of all the psychoanalytic wars I've witnessed in my lifetime, one school against the other, each claiming to be *the* (not just *a*) right way to do the work, the superior omniscience of different schools, the one who KNOWS. Bion lived through this atmosphere of righteous omniscience, a knowing that makes you feel right and too often violently so. In my book, *Rage* (2002) I suggest nothing has done more harm in human history than the sense of being right. We're right, you're wrong. During the Cold War I was afraid someone would trigger disaster by thinking he knew something he didn't.

Participant: Are you afraid that could happen now?

Mike: Not in the same way as there are more safeguards. But in our digital fast-speed world someone could break boundaries without sufficiently caring what might be triggered. For some, the more mayhem the better. I'm afraid certain kinds of stupidity and omniscience often go together.

Wilhelm Fliess's son, Robert, wrote a wonderful psychoanalytic trilogy, the third called *Symbols, Dreams and Psychosis* (1970) in which he called attention to the self-righteousness of the child abuser. He also associated a certain kind of mental blanking out with early trauma. There are many variations of these themes. Someone I worked with spoke of being raped while the rapist kept saying, "You're so soft" and feeling she loved it. A total lack of empathy for the pain one causes, physical and emotional. At the same time there are also abusers who feel gratified by the pain they cause. When I have worked with such people, I often found they were inflicting on victims some version of trauma and humiliation inflicted on them when they were helpless to do anything about it. A kind of doing to others what was done to them.

At the moment, related to this, I'm thinking of Walter Davis's (2003) play on Jon Benet Ramsey. He felt the father was the abuser, which may or may not be true. Davis took the liberty of writing what he thought was in the father's mind and portrayed him as a self-justifying abuser. He wrote it from the point of view of Jon Benet as an adult thinking about her life. She hadn't been killed but is now an adult on a psychoanalytic couch talking about her trauma. In a related, broader book, *Death's Dream Kingdom* (2006) he portrays America as a traumatized traumatizer and vice versa.

Participant: There's a book by Jack Katz called *Seductions of Crime* (1988) and in it is a chapter called "Righteous Slaughter." It says pretty much what you are saying now about hundreds of people who kill. It's quite remarkable.

There really is a lot of work out there on why we kill and who we are. And the work keeps growing. James Gilligan, a psychiatrist who worked with killers in jail wrote a book called *Violence: Reflections on a National Epidemic* (1997). He found early humiliation and shaming an important dynamic the murderer attempts to reverse (e.g., "now you feel what you did to me"). I remember a time when such reversal was called revenge, but Gilligan highlights the importance of shaming that often might be missed. Recently he co-authored a work with David Richards focusing on shame, guilt and violence in Shakespeare.

There was a moment in Graham Greene's *Brighton Rock* (1938) published two years after I was born and read two or three decades later that stayed with me with searing clarity. A man and woman are talking, feeling each other out as interest rises. And as his feelings and desire rise more and reach a certain point he takes out a gun (instead of you know what) and kills her. A sense is he was protecting himself from his own feelings and vulnerability. He became afraid. So this can be another side of violence: "I don't want to feel vulnerable, at the mercy of my feelings or the other's power. In a way, this is analogous to Bion's not wanting to be trapped by understanding, desire, or expectation. Not wanting to be trapped by feelings.

There are so many ways to feel trapped-and-or-free. The wisdom or sage culture has found ways of expressing this in psycho-spiritual ways that add to and sometimes transcend politics and everyday social life. It touches moments of self-recognition that open freeing dimensions. I am pulling lightly on an envelope that keeps opening. For example, living paradoxes: "I am and am not my mind. I am and am not by body. I am and am not myself." I don't want to be trapped by myself or any of these functions, fantasies, realities. I don't want to be trapped. To be trapped and free at the same time seems to be part of time. So many possibilities. Any capacity can trap you. Any capacity can open an abyss. Any capacity can open an avenue for the Holy Spirit in uplifting, beautiful, joyful ways. One moment Saint Paul expresses Grace not knowing where his mind or body are – there is just Grace Itself. In another moment he cries, "What a dreadful thing to fall into the hands of the living God."

Participant:	What about a patient who doesn't want to be trapped by the analysis?
Mike:	Well, I hope most people are like that.
Participant:	What if they want to go?
Mike:	(taking the part of the imaginary patient): "I'm going to get away from you and be free!"
Participant:	"You don't have the patience." So what do you say?
Mike:	You say whatever comes to you. Maybe you say, "Do you think it's so easy to be free by just

	getting away from me? How are you going to get away from yourself? You can get away from me, that's easy. But what are you going to do with the one you're with 24/7 all the days of your life?"
Participant:	[Brings up fear of the patient ending the analysis by ending himself, a final freedom] Do you have an intervention ... ?
Mike:	Suicide is not the answer! And murder isn't either. So, what were you going to say? If you can't kill yourself, what are you going to do?
Participant:	Get to know yourself.
Mike:	Knowing is one thing. Living with yourself another. They may or may not always go together. How do you live with yourself? How do you develop awakenings of capacities that enable you to live with yourself in a fuller, better way?
Participant:	You have to have someone help you tolerate your panic attacks.
Mike:	You need something, someone under you that can support you as you go through things. More opens, more rooms in the house. You see there's more to the house than you thought. It's not just understanding – it's living. It's also understanding but not just understanding.
Participant:	What if you were raised in a sadistic, sociopathic house so that if someone goes underneath you, you feel it's your obligation to destroy them?
Mike:	Well, then you go through the destruction. Here's a whip, here's a gun, here I am, the therapist: destroy me. Try to destroy me. But you can't destroy the psyche. How many times have I died this session? How many times have you killed me this session? Have I survived, have I not survived? If I haven't survived the session, maybe I'll come back three sessions from now. Give me a chance, let's give the process a chance.
Participant (James Pearl):	I was just thinking, shame can be supported.
Mike:	Yes – all affects need support and it makes for a bigger house. It makes for more room. There are different ways to have feeling. Different

ways to experience experience. It could be like this – *argh*! It could be something more melodious and open: Oh, wow, I didn't know you were here. Hi.

Even emptiness needs support – perhaps especially emptiness, creative emptiness. There are many kinds of destructive emptiness but creative emptiness is real too and deeply needed, a deep companion, often soul presence. If you've gone through analytic training you've had that space stuffed many times with all kinds of commands, rules, ideas, dogmas, threats. But you've likely felt the opening that comes when the psyche opens, when something that had been lost or filled or profoundly injured touches you and says, 'Here I am. We're here together, in this together." You and your wounds, improbabilities, deformations grow together, begin again and again. What do you and your psyche fill emptiness with and how does emptiness come to your rescue? A patient once said to me, "I'm stuffed with myself and what I think I'm doing here is becoming less stuffy." When Bion speaks about the unknown he wants to preserve and live a space where more can happen. I think, too, of Heidegger's "clearing" through which more enters existence. I suspect the Biblical phrase, "my cup runneth over" is a good example of filled-empty working in a positive way, like a good feed at the mother's breast – the emptiness before and the emptiness after. Can you practice being filled by emptiness with different qualities?

Of course there is more-less, too much-too little, positive-negative. But to add a good emptiness to an overstuffed psyche and therapy room can be a blessing. Waiting together can be a profound and giving experience. The Bible has a variety of words for emptiness, nothingness, abyss and its sibling chaos which were part of the "raw material" of creation as God trembled over the waters – and let there Be … and it was good. Rebbe Menachem Schneerson would say that God creates the universe from nothing every moment. Can you find that happening within you now? And now? Tao's emptiness is allied with fluidity, water, flow. Buddhist *sunyata* brings creative release, relief, appreciative living. Bion's "funny" remark that he writes to prevent someone who KNOWS from filling the space deepens and enlivens the more one dwells with it. Knowledge is great – know thyself, knowledge is power – K opens and helps invent all kinds of treasures – the computer I am writing on, for example, and the triple-edged digital world contact we all have for good and evil, including weapons that could scarcely be imagined thousands of years ago. But something in human beings propelled them to keep opening reality. And, at times, using some of the practices K brings can help you find the empty spot that can't be filled by anything. That gives you a special place to be and gives and gives. It allows domains to emerge that could not be felt before. It can be quite a discovery to bring forth by letting be.

On the negative side, one might feel less than, blame oneself for not being more, ashamed or even self-hating for lack. When a good emptiness enters your field of awareness you might feel it shouldn't be there and not want it. Little by little you may find ways to tolerate its coming and going, enjoy the relief it brings, feel lifted by its beauty and marvel at ways it allows things to happen that could not have happened otherwise. A life of thanks, appreciation and discovery.

And it has practical value as well. Sometimes when you're in an argument with someone you love and it gets worse and worse – shut up, be quiet. Are you fighting to be right, fighting for justice (in your terms), trying to right an injury or wrong that predates you, fighting out of pain? Can you put down your weapons and find a tiny bit of quiet mind, a hint of quietude, a little bit of the Shabbos point of your soul? How can you do this if you are hurt, angry, in pain, right, in need of justice? Yet a greater need of the moment may be a taste of peace, not war. A second's time out to feel your hara, but it could be other places.

Participant:	The what? The heart?
Mike:	Hara – a little below the navel.
Participant:	What's its function?
Mike:	It's harder to argue with someone when you breathe from your hara, you focus on a deeper center. Feeling your heart center can do it too. I suppose if you're a professional fighter you can fight from your hara. In the army they used to train you chest out belly in, just the opposite, breathing from a higher place, contracting the fullness of hara breath. If you feel yourself more deeply the drive to defend yourself and win settles down. In a way, you might say, you and the other begin to breathe together. Less military, more possibility.
Participant:	I do that in sessions sometimes. I'll put my finger on my belly button and just breathe.
Mike:	You give yourself and the other space where something else might happen.
Participant:	It's different from the I too.
Mike:	An opening for more life. Buddhism speaks of a third eye and Theodore Reik speaks of listening with a third ear. Opening the field beyond the will or need to control, perhaps birthing something new.

Bion affirms the value of an "empty space" many ways but fears he may be filling it with knowing and reason too. He recalls Swift's *Gulliver's Travels* where reason was associated with apes and humans suffered the unreasonable messes they made. An ironic thread runs through Bion's work as well as Swift's. If you want a quick taste of Swiftean irony read his little tract, *A Modest Proposal*, which suggests eating babies in response to the Irish potato famine. Swift is one of many spirits alive in Bion. Quite a blend, Swift's irony, Saint John of the Cross and Meister Eckhart's mysticism, blends of chakras-sephirot, energy centers and emotional nuclei we have no idea about in spite of all our ideas.

I see we are going overtime and it's time to stop for today. So in the spirit of the moment, "Wishing you all a Happy Lunacy and a Relativistic Fission." (Bion 1991, p. 378). "That's all folks!" To be continued ...

References

Bion, W. R. (1948). *Experiences in Groups: And Other Papers*. Routledge: London, 1991.

Bion, W. R. (1984). *Second Thoughts: Selected Papers on Psychoanalysis*. Routledge, London.

Bion, W. R. (1989). *Two Papers: The Grid and the Caesura*. Routledge: London, 2019

Bion, W. R. (1990). *Cogitations*. Routledge: London.

Bion, W. R. (1991). *A Memoir of the Future*. Routledge: London.

Davis, W. A. (2003). *An Evening with JonBenet Ramsey*. XLibris.

Davis, W. A. (2006). *Death's Dream Kingdom: The American Psyche Since 9–11*. Pluto Press: London.

Eigen, M. (1993). *The Electrified Tightrope*. Ed. A. Phillips. Routledge: London, 2004.

Eigen, M. (1998). *The Psychoanalytic Mystic*. London: Free Association Books.

Eigen, M. (1999). *Toxic Nourishment*. Routledge: London, 1991.

Eigen, M. (2002). *Rage*. Wesleyan University Press. Middletown, CT.

Eigen, M. (2004). *The Sensitive Self*. Wesleyan University Press. Middletown, CT.

Elkin, H. (1972). On selfhood and the development of ego structures in infancy. *Psychoanalytic Review* 59(3): 389–416. Collected in *On the Origin of the Self: The Collected Papers of Henry Elkin*. Ed. L Daws. Epis Press. Berkeley, CA., 2016.

Fliess, R. (1970). *Symbol, Dream and Psychosis*. International Universities Press: Madison, CT.

Ghent, E. (1990). Masochism, submission, surrender 1: Masochism as a perversion of surrender. *Contemp. Psychoanal* 26: 108–136.

Gilligan, J. (1997). *Violence: Reflections on a National Epidemic*. Vintage: New York.

Greene, G. (1938). *Brighton Rock*. Penguin Classics: New York, 1984

Katz, J. (1988). *Seductions of Crime: Moral and Sensual Attractions in Doing Evil*. Basic Books: New York.

Milner, M. (1987). *The Suppressed Madness of Sane Men: Forty-Four Years of Exploring Psychoanalysis*. Routledge: London.

Winnicott, D. W. (1986). *Home is Where We Start From: Essays by a Psychoanalyst*. W. W. Norton & Co.: New York, 1990.

Chapter 3

Tiny I-bits and Big Ones Too

[Working with Chapter 6 "Shame" in *Image, Sense, Infinities and Everyday Life*]

Our funny "I" has lots of ins and outs and ups-and-downs – inside out, outside in, upside down, downside up. Have you ever gotten tired of having or being an I? Our I can be so tiring – demanding this, not liking that, never good enough, always too good or any mixture you can think of. A patient once told me, "Without an I, I wouldn't be and yet my I stings me and I feel better without it." So many moments and mixtures. Freud spoke about a kind of observing I in the midst of a breakdown, watching oneself go to pieces. What or who is going to pieces and what or who is watching?

Philosophies talk about transcending the I, emptying oneself of the nagging ego. In the 1960s there was a strong emphasis on finding oneself, self-realization, fulfilling potential. Rollo May spoke of an I-am-I experience, a centering moment that brought to mind a translation of a biblical name of God as "I am that I am" or "I will be there." Confusion-opposition of I-God can be very tricky. In Kabbalah "What" or "That" can signify the Unknowable That Gives Birth to Everything. The Hindu Tat Tvam Asi – Thou Art That has a similar ring, whatever differences one emphasizes between East and West. In my early twenties, I valued Thomas Merton (1949) linking the secret of our identity with Divine Mercy (1949). I think of Job saying, "Yea, though You slay me yet will I trust You." And another passage, "What did Job see too wonderful to know." (Eigen, 1995, 2012).

Inflation-deflation runs deep in our psyche. When I was a kid I could not help noticing God was dog spelled backward and vice versa. As a grown-up I found the God-dog reversal-conjunction in Bion's work. Not only that, he tells us when he was a child he thought God's name was Arf-Arfer, as adults sounded like they were saying Arf-Arf-Arf when they were talking about God. The more one immerses in Bion's work, the more one may appreciate his dark humor, a kind of Swiftean irony. Indeed, he refers to *Gulliver's Travels* in some of his last sentences in one of his last books, when he depicts apes as reasonable and humans as – well, a mess (Bion, 1991).

As we all know, "I" can contract-expand, feel bigger-smaller, take many forms. I can identify with almost anything. I like to write Walt Whitman's "I contain multitudes" from *Song of Myself* as "I am multitudes." Don't

DOI: 10.4324/9781032658926-4

miss Bob Dylan's song, "I Contain Multitudes" (one of so many treasures on Google). And yes, I can get mixed up with God. "I am God" can take many forms just as Rimbaud's "I am another" can. As an adult, while studying Kabbalah I came across this children's song written by Rabbi Yosef Goldstein (quoted with permission of his son, Rabbi Levy Goldstein):

Hashem is here, Hashem is there
Hashem is truly everywhere!
Up, up, down, down,
Right, left, and all around!
Here, there and everywhere
That's where He can be found!

Hashem literally means the Name, but it is unpronounceable and even unknowable. It gives birth to everything and is in everything but can you find it? Is it localizable? Can you sense it, feel it, know it in some way? Mystics speak of a union with God. Is it a union that is always there although so often we may also be and feel "separate"? Both-and, and-or, either-or?

In some of my work, I speak of a distinction-union structure (1986) that is part of experience. And our own I – can you locate it? Where is the I? Some speak of a belly I, heart I, head I. So many functions, capacities, states. An I am I experience can be awakening. If joyful, joy can be a reference point for moments of existence. But so often it is threatened and one inhabits sorrow, pain, loss, anger, rage, fear, terror, horror. Winnicott speaks of the primal agonies of an infant. Saint Paul's "God is love" and "What a dreadful thing to fall into the hands of the living God" are both sobering and tantalizing. In *Attention and Interpretation* (Chapter 2, 1970) Bion writes of a catastrophic link that holds personality together, a work he refers to near the end of his life in *A Memoir of the Future*. In what ways can a catastrophic link organize personality? I'm thinking of outbreaks of war today and surges of local violence, including teenagers shooting up schools and churches as if violence is some way of achieving a sense of momentary cohesion. There's a lot of violent "I am" ing in the face of threatened I-loss.

Freud wrote "the ego is its own ideal," a phrase with many possible meanings, including the I as an ideal I, narcissistic I, or something ever growing that can never grow enough. You can make up and discover your own meanings. He depicts it as both hallucinatory and reality testing, hallucinating wish-fulfilling states and realistically problem solving. Ego as structure, agent, function. On a quasi-phenomenological level, it can be depicted as changing states in myriad ways, e.g., inflated-deflated, proud-ashamed, self-love/self-hate. Patients depict aspects of this in dreams, e.g. a balloon flying high, popping, blown around by the wind helplessly falling formlessly to the ground, one moment omnipotent, the next impotent. Kohut wrote of a grandiose self and a shrunken inferior self with many useful clinical variations. Jung depicted the evolution of a deeper self allied with a sense of wholeness.

Once when a religious person was telling me what a shit he was he suddenly stopped and said, "But God created shit too!" He went on to wonder if God created defecation and deficiency in general to remind us we were not God but one of God's wonders. It would not be surprising if an unconscious sense of shit as divine might be part of perverse fecal worship or self-overestimation. A patient smeared himself with shit saying he felt it healing. Another smeared himself to demonstrate how lowly he was. Still, another patient felt a chasm between his being god and shit falling on him and out of him. How to reconcile high-low? Freud associated aspects of anal experience with creativity, making something. Bion used the term "evacuation" to depict ridding oneself of potential feeling. Jung wrote of the evolution of a deeper self allied with evolution of wholeness. Our psychic palette is breathtaking.

Participant (Jim Nicholls):   I think of Jesus as part of a Trinity with a sense that God became a servant, Jesus as God the servant.

I think, too, of the biblical sense of Israel as God's servant. These kinds of phrases touch a dimension of experience in which we serve each other. When we apply this to ourselves we usually take it as "self-serving," selfish, but there is a deeper meaning, a kind of invitation to be good to ourselves, a soul-servant, a servant of the depths of being. There are many "service" professions, including those that offer serious and sincere care for human beings, life in general and our planet. I feel lucky that we are part of this, caring for people, working with psychic depths and as Freud suggested to Fliess, engaged in potentially helpful transformation processes. There is beauty in this kind of learning and serving, unconscious to unconscious, psyche to psyche.

There are times I feel our whole body breathing, blood vessels, cells, pores – all breathing, expanding-contracting. I think of Lacan's phrase for the opening-closing of the unconscious, "pulsations from the slit." Or one of William Blake's depictions of creativity growing from the pulsation of an artery. Taoism associates such rhythms with existence and life. Bion's notation, F in O, points to a kind of Faith as an opening to unknown reality (O), a rhythm of faith. Freud speaks of deep psychic rhythms that can work well or poorly. Psychic pulsations.

Implicit in Freud's ego as its own ideal are ways one fails to be the envisioned ideal and often shame associated with falling short and being less than. In one extreme form, "I'll always be ashamed because I can't live up to my own ideal. I can't be the ideal me. I am my own ideal and ashamed because I can never be it." Or in another moment, "If I am my own ideal I'm ashamed of my limitations. I can never live up to being me." Or even more extreme, "I can never be me." I am and am not myself. I am and am not me. One can be ashamed of almost anything if shame is working.

Psychic or psychophysical size is one dimension often used as a comparison measure, e.g., the spectrum small-big. Shame is associated with feeling-being too little or big, including nothing-everything. One feels invisible or sticks out too much. One's face may lose color or become highly charged. Psychic minification-magnification takes many "forms."

I'm wondering if Trump is an example of inflation pushing past inner-outer barriers, a kind of grandiose blotting out spectrums of limitations. On the other hand, I think of a man in the back of the temple during High Holy Day services banging his chest, saying over and over, "I'm nothing, I'm nothing." And the rabbi turns around and says, "Look who's calling himself a nothing."

Does one have to become like Trump to avoid persecuting oneself for not being enough? Does one have to inflate oneself to blot out perception of deficiency? Or can one feel the deep freedom humility can bring, not having to be one's own ideal, but appreciating and living with what a flawed, challenged mortal can be and do? There appear to be negative ways of using almost any capacity.

During the 1960s there was much emphasis on self-actualization psychology. One is always actualizing oneself, never fully actualized. One cannot fully be one's potential because the latter is an ongoing process. Franz Kafka must have felt something like this when he described his life as "an incomplete moment." In a way, there's nothing to live up to because you are in the process of growing. A word some might have used is "unfolding." As long as you are alive the process continues. There are ways that psychic growth does not stop and there are many ways to grow. A patient said, "I feel I am growing inside but can't say how. It's something happening, opening, deepening but I do not have words for this."

A so-called learning-disorder client wrote a best seller. Another who was given medication as a child for Attention Deficit Disorder became a terrific artist and took himself off medication. He had been shamed in school for not living up to his potential. Teachers kept saying, "If you work harder, you can do it." It was not "hard work" that was the answer but discovering other ways of working, finding and respecting the ways one did work and how to work with it. One may be learning deficient in some ways according to certain criteria but may have other ways or organizing and processing experience. It is important to learn and grow into what one *can* do, catch on to and work with ways your mind and being work and partner with your gifts and experience. I remember Isaac Bashevis Singer (1991) quoted as saying, "Every human being, even if he is an idiot, is a millionaire in emotions." We are unbelievably rich in experiencing and need to discover how to partner with it.

When Bion spoke about terminal cancer he asked what does "terminal" mean? What can a person do in the time he has? "What *can* you do? What is it you *can* do while you're here?" Along this line, he asked, no matter how damaged, "What *are* you good for?" (A link to what Bion said about terminal cancer: https://www.youtube.com/watch?v=r68oInRsFEI). He spoke about finding the wavelength that can still open experience. I have a feeling he meant this for one's dying moment as well. It may be Bion had terminal cancer without knowing it. He passed away shortly after discovering he was ill at the age of 82 in 1979. I think of Tolstoi's story, *The Death of Ivan Ilyich,* when the dying Ivan feels profoundly alive for the first time. I think, too, of Winnicott's prayer written in his notebook 1970 the year he died, now published 2016 in *The Collected Works,* "Oh, God, may I be alive when I die." Of course it's good to be alive when one's living too.

Something in me has always felt, as far back as I can remember, that we are all gifted. We have a phrase, "the gift of life." We can make that a capital L, "the gift of Life." Whether big L or small l a sense of life runs through us, permeates our beings, which is one reason feeling dead can be so awful. Literature is filled with myths, stories, references to being dead while alive. My sense is the deadness would not be so awful if life, unconscious memory of aliveness, or something like an inchoate, formless intimation of what life can be or do were not there. The phrase "the living dead" suggests deadness would not be so bad if one were not living it. A special gift granted to some is the ability to express what it feels like to be dead while alive in ways that move others. There are so many kinds of gifts and ways to share them, including learning to share them with oneself. There are many people who do not know they are gifted, who do not sense what they have been given or can feel and be. I don't mean gifts that can be translated into money and recognition but something intrinsic, that exists in itself for its own sake, breathes and circulates in its own ways.

We have so many spectrums of binaries that both express and confine multitudes of possibilities and fine lines that invisibly run through them. Spectrums of binaries crisscrossing all sorts of ways. We are all so limited and flawed, so grandiose and ashamed, victimized by hostile omniscience and self-evacuation. Everything is new, nothing is new, this moment never was before, this moment always is. If you can do nothing else but breathe, you have a chance. Someone I work with tells me, "All I have is breathing. I am so grateful I discovered breathing, in-feelings, out-feelings, a quiet flow all through my body-being. I feel for the first time I am permeating myself." Another person began to feel that "breathing never stops. The whole universe is breathing."

Her feeling made me feel life is breathing, even though I know there is life before breath. There is quite some ambiguity here. Did God create the world with word or breath or something else entirely? Torah says, "The soul is in the blood." Does that mean some form of interpenetrating circulation? I have a very deep sense of cellular breath and circulation.

Are we always detouring? I sometimes feel my whole life is a detour with a deep, interpenetrating heart. Freud spoke of permeable-rigid structures-tendencies. We continue to amplify hints he gave (which imprinted him from pre-antiquity) about outside-inside, intrinsic-extrinsic and what I sometimes "describe" as distinction-union.

Taking a little Freud dip, "I am my own ideal – I will never be my own ideal. I'll never become it. I am it. Will I, can I be it? I'm not it, yes-no, plus-minus." Or another pairing with profound meaning and repercussions: We're all God – We're all shit. A patient once said, "I'm just a piece of shit." Then followed with, "What would the universe be without shit? I like the smell of shit." Jung once dreamt of God shitting on the universe. Bion liked spelling God backward: dog. He remarked as a child when adults talked about God he thought they were saying, "Arf, Arf, Arf," and he called God Arf Arfer. In New York City we are required to pick up our dog-do, bag and dispose of it. Freud commented we sometimes have trouble telling the difference between gold and shit – the two seem inextricably fused and opposed in our psyche. An oddity of language that gold has god in it as well as go and old? My father used to smoke Old Gold.

Participant:	The God-dog link used to be called "the dog collar."
Mike:	Because you are a God-servant. Fetch! Fetch! Fetch salvation!
Participant:	Like a halo that drops down on my neck strangling me.
Mike:	Oh, no! I'm suffocating! Set me free, set me free!
Participant:	Strangled by the halo.
Mike:	Hanging by the halo. I'm hung by my halo.
Participant:	What the halo's going on?
Mike:	Halo and Hardy! One thing about Bion, his language is packed not just with opposites but whole spectrums of meldings. Language is so stiff and so melted at the same time and so much stuff that's in it corresponds to psychic states. I'm not sure when I first saw this – I wonder, possibly before language if there is a before language. Just a sense of things. I do remember as a child meditating on the pairing of "Look before you leap" and "He who hesitates is lost." It began to dawn on me that adults spoke in opposites and fusions. What words pertain to what state, moods and moments? A sense of varying capacities, tendencies and states has grown with me. Twists and turns, nuances, variations –sometimes we speak of a river, a flow, or musical themes. Jung used to say of varied possibilities, "Throw it in the soup." Quite some soups the ingredients of life keep making.

At this moment in history, we seem to be undergoing a breakdown of truth and trust. It may be that truth and trust go together and always suffer partial breakdowns, sometimes worse or better. Different groups claim their way of seeing things is the truth or more truthful than other perspectives and too often violence results. Whose "truth" is better? I've written before about the first moments I was in a private room with Bion for a session. He was taller than I yet in some way I felt he was under me, supporting me, supporting my psyche, something akin to vibrations of the word understand, to stand under. To stand under and give support, serving psychic growth. One can sense a certain humility and openness in contrast to dominance.

There are so many positive-negative uses of capacities, all kinds of mixtures, reversals, antagonisms. Freud spoke of megalomania, Kohut grandiosity, enormous inflation and self-overestimation in contrast and tension with its counterpart, a pervasive sense of inferiority, shame – as with so many functions and systems, expansion-contraction in myriad keys. Each of these states has its survival and enlivening aspects as well as dangers. Often danger is part of aliveness.

People write of mental ego – body ego, mental self–body self. Husserl wrote of a transcendent as well as psychological ego, Jung a transcendent function. Transcendence-immanence: dual moments. We are citizens of multiple realities. Freud wrote of a state's reversal into its opposite. In a session, someone said, "One moment I feel I am living forever, the next time has me by my tail." Can we develop a sustained yet modulated appreciation for the life of moments? Back-forth, in-out seem to be basic elements of experience.

The Biblical Job is an amazing archetypal portrayal of movement to a zero point and rebirth through a new kind of awareness, at once beyond, through and with oneself, a term in which one and self combine in the presence of multiplicity, a kind of emptying out, poverty and richness never-ending. Ideal feeling has its moments but so does just plain ordinary me. I remember a fun combination in a Hindu story about a disciple meeting the master after a long absence and the disciple is all bandaged up. The guru asks what happened." The main replied, "Remember you used to tell me to say to myself, 'I am God, I am God?' Well a man on an elephant was coming toward me and I was in the middle of the street, so I kept saying to myself, 'I am God, I am God.' And he trampled all over me." "Schmuck," the guru said. "He's God too."

There's a transcendent context to our lives and an immanent context that we live through. An ideal feeling runs through it but it's not the only feeling. It's important to learn how to work with it and do good work together. But the bandaged man also symbolizes the collapse and morass that is part of the rhythm of existence. Without quite realizing it, Job was, in part, trapped between vocalized explosion and implosive collapse and discovered a new kind of moment that furthered his sense of life. Defiance, opposition, and collapse can function as survival mechanisms if we learn how to work with them. In the middle of Goethe's Faust upon learning of Margaret's tragedy, what does Faust do? He falls into profound sleep which helps him begin to recover and regroup. He could not endure the pain of tragic loss and fell unconscious as a kind of escape yet healing gesture enabling him to go on. He comes back and eventually has a similar kind of learning as Voltaire's Candide: Tend your garden.

Wishful thinking on the part of two French and German writers? France and Germany fighting each other for centuries? Like the Spanish and Portuguese? War after war, it never seemed to stop. By the end of the Second World War fighting between European countries had been going on for a thousand years or more. Tend your gardens? Like Adam?

Participant: Garden is a central symbol in Islam, associated with paradise, but also all the good growth of creation, the flower of the soul, a place of God's presence.

Participant: In the garden there's a snake.
Mike: And a commandment, "Thou shall not."
Participant: Thou shall not or your out.
Mike: Existential writers like Rollo May wrote about the expulsion as a growth of consciousness.
Participant: Some call it the fall up rather than the fall down.
Mike: It could be a fall in all directions, an omnidirectional fall.
Participant: It could go both ways, blameless and grandiose. I did nothing wrong and look what happened. A rising consciousness of loss, kicked out for no good reason together with a rising consciousness of grandiosity, two sides of the shock of shame. If you do something wrong are you really going to learn?
Mike: I'm wondering if a way of putting two sides of the spectrum might be grandiose and self-evacuative. I'm thinking of Trump and his brother, something I wrote about in "Psychopathy in Everyday Life" (2016a). Trump needed, went after and won his father's approval, his brother didn't. Trump outdid his father as a real estate magnate and more. His older brother, Fred, became an alcoholic and died halfway through his life in his forties. Flying planes was his passion. Their father had a negative response to this and turned to the younger brother, Donald, to advance his business ambitions. Donald claims as a result of Fred's life, he never drinks liquor. An image I get is Donald's form of flying is, partly, an inflated ego in contrast with his brother's deflation. Mary Trump (2020), Fred's daughter, exposed the shadow side of her family and, particularly, Donald's makeup. Mary Trump, as far as I can tell, was 16 when her father died and had seen and lived

through family injury and meanness. Donald, among other things, tried to have his dying father's will changed so that Mary and her brother would be excluded from the inheritance. In some ways Donald's brother Fred lived out a self-evacuative aspect of the psyche and Donald some forms of inflated grandiosity.

One has to put up with a lot of suffering. Even the intensity of one's life feeling can be painful. In the Bible story, there appears to be a lot of problematic negativity in paradise. And in our lives, there is no end to the care our gardens need. As ancient Greek literature tells us, love is a problematic challenge filled with wounds.

We are not only polarities but spectrums of possibility, so many waters doing so many things at once, multi-directional flows-and-rigidities. Look at our body – more rigid backbone and flowing blood, multiple systems doing different things and creating an amazing something we tend to call a whole, if we mean by "whole" continuing processes not a finished "totality." We are challenged to learn to partner with ourselves, swing back to forth on hinges that are not too squeaky, tight or loose. Navigate the states, nurture and culture them, negotiate them. It's so easy to feel flooded, too much, too little.

Keep a notebook. Marion Milner would note the most significant moment (s) in her day. Jot a few points of significance. Even if you are a dead person, so much happens in a day or an hour, so many variations of deadness. And if you are both dead and alive note what happens inside you for an hour. Nothing stays the same. Woops – I hear someone saying nothing *is always* the same. But no, nothing varies too.

Participant: How does one partner with and grow a capacity?
Mike: You're going to have to work on that one.
Participant: How does one work on it?
Mike: No formula here, no one way. You think about it, feel it, taste it. Try to build up tolerance for a little more. There can be moments of Grace. You don't know where it comes from or how it gives you a whole new frame of reference and you say, "Oh my God, I never felt this before." Or it can be, "Uh-oh, the bad thing is happening, can I tolerate it a little more?" Kind of like a psychic gymnasium – can I do one more lift, one more pushup, one more bend? Can I take a little bit more of myself? How much of myself can I take this moment, and this, and … ? Hanging in there and little by little building up more tolerance for oneself.

On what seems like another track, Jung speaks of an inner marriage. How can you marry yourself, to what extent, with what quality? What can that mean?

I tend to speak of learning how to partner yourself a little better. One of my models is learning how to play piano and practicing the scales. Bion emphasizes building tolerance for your experience, another moment of experience, a little more tolerance and a little more. Maybe just sit, like Buddha. And feel before acting, feel a little more, and a little more. You don't know where it is going to go. Do this over time and your capacity gradually begins to build in other dimensions as well. You don't want to overly tax yourself so that you go nuts, get high blood pressure, or stick your head in the oven. But you can try to take a little more before trying to switch off.

Doing things that touch you can help. Something you love to read, a movie. Maybe watch Beatrice Beebe's mother-infant movies and sensitize yourself to moment-to-moment shifts of nuances of states. Or just sitting and feeling, and feeling a little more. You can gain a lot, too, tolerating sensations exercise creates, a walk, a run, stretching. You can practice taking your time a little more. You have something like a light switch that can turn a feeling on or off. Respect it. There is much to learn in transitions of turning off and on. Don't be too hard on yourself if you have to shut down. There will be more moments, more times.

Participant: Can you do a full sit-up or half a pushup?

Mike: Now in my mid-eighties I can sometimes run for three or more hours and do one hundred pushups a day. But there are times I need to stop and rest, change pace, let go, give up for the moment. No one time fits all. Respect the moment, care for what is happening now. As John Milton writes at the end of his poem, "On His Blindness" – "They also serve who only stand and wait." He was wondering how to work with and make the most of his disability. I've come to deeply value, a kind of openness to and waiting on the unknown. As Bion emphasizes, there is much to gain by doing-feeling whatever you *can* do or feel rather than punish yourself with what you can't. Lying in bed before sleeping or a little while after waking can be wonderful moments of being.

Participant: I sometimes think Gandhi took to his spinning wheel because he could not handle what was going on. It gave him a deeper sense of calm and well-being and perhaps much more.

Mike: Yes, he had a profound and touching relation to his spinning wheel, which gave him a deeper sense of being. Sometimes, if I can't take any more of myself, I go for a run or play the piano and other dimensions open. I suspect Gandhi's spinning wheel functioned similarly, perhaps like a musical instrument. You learn how to work with yourself. On and off throughout his life he wanted to be a doctor. Although that never happened his dedication to healing life was a constant.

Participant: He spun cotton for hours. That was part of his movement/protest against British goods. He walked a lot of miles and he spun cotton.

Mike: There's no one else with you all the time, only you. I'm a believer in finding what works for you. Weaving is a primordial activity and art. Pottery is a peaceful but constructive use of one's hands. Sometimes when I think of weaving or pottery I think of a baby discovering and using its hands. Hand-to-mouth movement may be part of the background of the art of cooking.

No end to it. We have so many things to try to make outlets for ourselves to divert and/or use the aggression. Sports, art, building. Music worked for me for a good part of my life. I've been musical from a very early age, thank God.

Participant: It works the other side of the brain. You know the phrase limbic music.

Mike: Music is all through you. The ancients spoke of music of the spheres and we can speak of the music of the psyche. Kabbalah uses "spheres" to designate different psycho-bio-spiritual capacities and functions. Freud used the word "scene" derived from theater to depict aspects of dream-life and psychic movements. When I think of Gandhi spinning I can't help thinking of autistic spinners who whirl around like a dervish till the bad world is gone and a better feeling comes. Or my love of spinning tops as a child and merry-go-rounds, many varieties of spinning, including getting dizzy, faint or spinning with joy. Round, round, round we go, where we stop nobody knows. Spinning world or self, mixing familiarity with mystery.

I'm thinking of the State Psychiatrist moving from pacification to transformation (Bion 1991, Ch. 17, p. 81). When he first appears he says his job is to keep order, pacify. Don't wake the place with a scream, give him a shot of morphine. Keep the psyche quiet. Moments later Bion brings up Transformation as a process, a way of life or part of living and the State Psychiatrist turns on a dime and says, "Why, even I am transformed." He launches into a soliloquy about death and creativity, dying out-coming back, falling slack and renewal: Life's movements between pacification-Transformation and much more.

The State Psychiatrist did not mean Buddhist *sunyata* – emptiness – by pacify. And likely did not mean peace within self or nations. He meant something more like shut up, don't let the demons out, quiet, no disturbance. In a pacified state you're less likely to kill someone or injure yourself. However, in another moment you might become a warrior and knock someone out. How do we do justice to all the states that rise and fall and have their moments? In one or another situation, they may all play a role in survival.

Participant: Many psychotherapists discourage patients from bringing objects or things they would play with because of a bias towards articulating what is going on in their head.

Mike: There's no one way of working. In play therapy one works with these objects as giving expression to oneself. To make use of Winnnicott, one might view therapy as a psychic playground. Lots of "objects" can swim into view and play varied roles in psychic movement.

Participant: Freud's great-granddaughter had a sculpture that was a presence in Freud's office. She said all his little figurines have spots where they're worn down by his playing with them.

Participant: Weren't those on his desk?

Mike: His desk was filled with treasures, one of his favorites Athena. He was in contact with ages past, the buried, the found, symbols of the living psyche.

Participant: I saw his old office in Vienna when I was there in 1973. The old rugs, the rug on the couch, the figurines on the desk – it felt so primitive, another world.

Mike: The burgeoning figures were like cellular life of the psyche. Perhaps primitive meaning primary, early, prime, came from Austria-Hungary, migrated from Vienna in 1923, now and our modest apartments and then house were bathed by Asian rugs that must have been very similar to ones that helped center and enrich Freud. The several Asian rugs in my own house now add to my feeling at home. When you say "another world" I feel like saying a world alive with psyche.

Participant: And a dog was there too.

Mike: Life was there. You're a therapist. And as I look around the room I see therapist after therapist. And you could do therapy like no other. I feel I can say that about all the therapists I see: you can do therapy like no one else. Take in everything you see other people do, learn wherever you can, whatever works for you. But you have your own quirks and you do it your own way. Respect that, because that's a creative point, a link with yourself that you can use, that you can develop as it develops you.

Look what Freud offered – it wasn't just or only a blank screen. His office was filled – as he was – with so many creatures of the psyche to draw from, develop, share. So many aspects of the psyche to grow with and a sense of the unknown and mystery giving birth.

Participant: Perhaps it was his wish to be a blank screen but he just couldn't do it. Maybe it was, in some way, an idealized state.

Mike: Blank can have multiple meanings. There is a kind of blankness that is a painful state that plagues a life, a negative emptiness akin to aborting oneself, unable to live a life. There is, too, momentary or long-term "blanking out" in face of pain. Robert Fliess, son of Wilhelm, linked this with resurgence of aspects of childhood trauma. The psyche is in a position of trying to communicate longstanding emotional pain at the same time as trying to mute it. At the same time there is a kind of creative blankness or emptying out, opening to unknown processes and possibilities. In contrast with self-aborting dimensions, there are ways we give birth to ourselves all life long. We speak of filled-empty moments leaving room for more to happen, a metaphor saying there are ways you can always start again. For example, I might feel or even say something like, "Oh, I sucked that session. But maybe next session I'll be better. Let's try again. Our rebirth is always in process. Bion spoke of always being embryonic in some way. So even if you or I or we messed up this moment, embryonic growth is still possible, likely necessary. Unconscious-to-unconscious, psyche-to-psyche processes keep happening in a plethora of ways. The image of a screen or mirror is often used – we are screens and mirrors for each other and ourselves. Often I am a very mixed, uneven screen and if a mirror I certainly have cracks (it is no accident being "cracked" can be a reference to different kinds and degrees of madness, whether humorous or devastating). There are moments blank can open more than it closes. I remember a writing-drawing tablet when I was a child that erased everything by pulling a transparent plastic cover. I suppose I could have been devastated by such sudden and total loss but I felt joy in being able to write or draw something new. Decades later I read Freud's account of traces left on the "mystic writing pad" after erasure and the therapy literature about going backward-forward at the same time. Freud was keen on sensing psychic rhythms. Find your own inner essence. Be a good screen for yourself. Even if it may seem certain blocks and damage may never go away, be assured there are ways psychic streams keep flowing. Building tolerance for mixed states and "news of difference" (Bateson, 1979).

I had a patient who had a self-erasing mind. She used the word erase in deep ways, erasing herself, traces of self. She felt it as part of her mind, a mental function that erased self-feeling. It was a terrible state. At the same time, it seemed to partly clean her out making a clearing for something further. In a way Freud's "blankness" was a kind of opening. Bion's F in O also conveys an open attitude, receptivity to the creative unknown, perhaps even a kind of creative waiting on the unknown, an opening to the forever fresh. Bion and Husserl, in their special ways, have a feel for starting fresh. I'm sure many of you have valued moments when you let the unknown create. There are ways the unknown is always creating us. In what ways can we partner with the unknown?

Bion had many models for psychic processes. In his late work, he drew one model from Yom Kippur, the Day of Atonement, which he wrote at-onement, O. At-onement with oneself. He tended to link O with unknown emotional reality. I also like Openness or Opening. Marion Milner liked re-writing Bion's O as 0 (zero), drawing on creative emptiness from a fusion of Buddhist *sunyata* and biblical creation stories (chaos, no-thing). Balint wrote of "an harmonious interpenetrating mix-up" and Winnicott (2016) wrote of an incommunicado core – the two combining a kind of essential aloneness and interpenetrating connectivity. Much can be said about both and their variable functions. I once had a patient who said, "My autism saved me." Yes, saved by autism, an alone place to feel self and reach out from. We may not know what's doing what when. For example, guilt, shame and fear can be civilizing and/or paralyzing. Too much-too little and with what quality has been pondered for thousands of years. Autism is usually thought of as a shell but it also can be a creative opening.

One of my Trump fantasies rotates around his inflated chest. I remember soldiers trained to have chest out – stomach in, very different from the belly relaxation I was encouraged to have in body therapies. The assertive, inflated chest seemed to push past shame, guilt or fear In contrast with Trump's brother's sense of shame, Donald oriented to attack the other, Fred Jr. to attack oneself. It might sound far-fetched to view Fred's death a suicide, but it was a result of alcoholism. Donald's manner, in contrast was a way of saying, "I will not kill myself." Or maybe even, "Better you than me." Of course, this is a picture of mine. Who knows what bits and pieces of pain are held together by inflated cohesion. A kind of family division of labor between inflation-deflation. It is one of many paradoxes that alcohol which may lighten the load, make one feel good, offset the bad feeling, raise one's spirits, can kill one with its toxicity. On a broader scale, much thought has been given to how feelings and attitudes are divided and function within families.

There is persistent pain in life and happy points too. One of my happy points is here (pointing to the center of chest), yet someone in a session yesterday spoke about the same spot as a center of agony. When he got up in the morning and went to sleep at night the same place I liked was awful for him. Since I was a little child I was aware that different people experienced different pleasures and pains, joys and agonies in different ways and places, as well as similar ones too. I knew this just by noting differences of positive and negative feelings from people in my own family, let alone friends and neighbors. When much older I learned about the neurology of pleasure-pain points and waves as well as systems of foci in yoga and kabbalah. So many streams through us so many ways. The person I was just speaking about, who goes to sleep and wakes up with a miserable feeling in the center of his chest, has moments of beauty on and off throughout the day. This same man writes beautiful poetry. Agony and beauty can mix and turn into moving music and art. When he is active during the day he experiences variable states yet on waking and going to sleep horror hits. I think of the biblical David describing how close and far God can feel, the agony of absence and bliss of Presence. I wonder about my patient's difficulty saying hello and goodbye to himself in moments of transition.

So many people have persistent pain points. My patient often described himself as an "idealist". I could not help thinking a paradoxical result of being one's own ideal is that one is persistently in pain because one can't fulfill that ideal, and likely no one else can either. Perhaps in Trump's case, grandiosity tried to fill the gap and in his brother's case, the gap was too overwhelming. In my patient's case, creative work acted as a bridge and sharing.

Phyllis Meadow's (2003) last book has beautiful passages on just being a human being, a mortal. Not the grandiosity of psychoanalysis or other omniscient games, but just accepting the package and doing what you can with what you may have. Psychoanalysis has done a lot to acknowledge and work with the god point one will never be, the I that I will never be, Working with I am that I am. Becoming a little freer from the tyranny of self-idealization. Since we often work in counterparts, self-idealization and self-persecution tend to go together, divided and distributed in many ways. Persistent high points and pain points. Our amazing imagination has tried to give this expression mythically, e.g., heaven-hell, expressions of emotional moments. In the chapter "Shame" I write of "A persistent pain point one tries to wash away with idealized feeling as it brings one down" (2016b, p. 65). In this case, idealized feeling tries to make us feel good in face of the thing that's making us feel bad. Part of Melanie Klein's (1946) genius are depictions of possible ways ideal feeling tries to make the bad feeling go away, how they split and combine to form myriad emotional possibilities.

One thing we learned in psychoanalysis is when you are in the throes of an ideal feeling keep an eye on the other side too. You don't have to spoil the moment – there is much to be gained from relishing its taste and work. But don't be surprised when the drop comes and the other side asserts its need and power. Be ready to work with the negative call when it asserts itself. Both positive and negative seeds have their value if one learns how to grow with them.

"The other side" is one of Kaballah's terms for evil, often depicted as a shell around a holy spark. Jung wrote of alchemy as a kind of model for the transformation of base elements to something better and, like Freud, opened possibilities for better use of our energies. Freud depicted sublimation as a kind of "defense" that made constructive use of what could be destructive energy or psychic forces. In spiritual writings, sublimation often flows from love and wisdom channeling and transforming our use of capacities for the better. A perennial issue is how to work with ourselves, partner our capacities in ways that are less destructive.

Klein (1946) delineates splitting and moving toward ambivalence. Idealization trying to wash away bad feeling can be one example of splitting. One might try to get rid of hate by projecting it into others. At the same time, one might get into trouble by over-idealizing other or self. In moving toward ambivalence (ambi-valence), we may be more able to tolerate disparate states and learn how to work with them. A course of growth is building tolerance for our multi-valence psychic realities. Bion spoke of building the capacity to suffer our feelings, work with, not just evacuate or destruct. In important ways, psychoanalysis teaches us to use psychic binocular (not just monocular) vision. I like using the term multi-ocular. I think, perhaps, of a multi-eyed Buddha viewing reality from many perspectives rather than getting trapped in monocular egoism. Another image might be an infinite heart. We have two physical eyes but using Bion's term multiple O-eyes. From time immemorial, as individuals and groups, we have seen how dangerous we can be and try to discover, learn, practice ways to minimize harm to ourselves and others. How can we be ourselves and keep multiple eyes on ourselves at the same time? A profound need for a capacity can stimulate its growth (Straus, 1966).

We try to wash away a persistent pain point with all kinds of things as it brings us down. I suspect the latter to be an ingredient of the sense of unworthiness one tries to cleanse. You often find this in the Vedas – an urge to cleanse the sin, cleanse the unworthiness. The psychoanalytic approach is a little different involving respect for each of the states we work with. Let the pain speak. What is it trying to convey? What are our self-attacking movements trying to tell us? Like the writers of myths, we are story-tellers, seeking the stories inherent in each individual we work with as well as ourselves. Often it is more accurate to speak of persistent pain points rather than a singular one. So many hurt babies, wounds, agonies each with many stories. Our pains are alive, akin to so many wounded babies seeking better ways into life. We mentioned the multi-edged work of idealized feeling that gives and steals at the same time. One can sometimes go more deeply into the states that stop one from living. They are filled with life of their own. What are they aching to tell us? They can contribute to creativity and more subtle living with oneself.

Empty, blank, open, a possibility of starting again and again. The work of healing-birthing doesn't stop. I've often mentioned Pierre-Janet who would try to create dialogical movement with persecutory hallucinations-delusions, entering conversation with relentless self-accusers. Bion uses the term "evacuation" in trying to get rid of bad feelings. M. Klein delineates a function of projection as an attempt to diminish internal attack. One function of psychoanalytic work is to increase respect for psychic complexity and possibility. You don't have to get rid of yourself in order to survive yourself. You don't have to act out all the bad parts to diminish pressure. You can build the capacity to tolerate our messy psyche and find ways of processing and living with experience that works for you. The process has many nooks and crannies and keeps growing. Respect – an important ingredient in working with our makeup, in working with ourselves. There are times – many – it can get very trying and tricky. Suppose a therapist asks what is your inner devil saying to you now. You say the answer is "Thou shalt be God!" What kind of God, what kind of devil, neither of us know where we will go from here but a deep sense grows and teaches, psyche will tell us more. At the moment I'm thinking of the presence-absence rhythms in the Psalms. God is closer-farther from the psalmist who longs for God's presence, juxtapositions of wonder, anguish, beauty. The deep dialogue in the Psalms is going on today moment to moment in our practice, our psyche, our world. In some sense, we are both guest and home in our lives. Part of our job is becoming a better guest, a better home for yourself and by contagion and hard work for others.

References

Bateson, G. (1979). *Mind and Nature*. New York: E.P. Dutton.

Bion, W. R. (1970). *Attention and Interpretation*. London: Routledge.

Bion, W. R. (1991). *A Memoir of the Future*. London: Routledge.

Eigen, M. (1995). *Reshaping the Self*. London: Routledge.

Eigen, M. (2012). *Kabbalah and Psychoanalysis*. London: Routledge.

Eigen, M. (2016a). Psychopathy in Everyday Life. *The Psychoanalytic Review* 103(6): 729–742

Eigen, M. (2016b) *Image, Sense, Infinities and Everyday Life*. London: Routledge.

Klein, M. (1946). Notes on some schizoid mechanisms. Eds. M. Klein, P. Heimann, S. Isaacs, and J. Riviere. *Developments in Psycho-Analysis*. London: Hogarth Press, 1952.

Meadow, P. (2003). *The New Psychoanalysis*. Washington, DC: Rowman and Littlefield.

Merton, T. (1949). *New Seeds of Contemplation*. Reprinted by New Directions, New York 2007.

Singer, I. B. (1991). NY Times obituary by E. Pace. https://www.nytimes.com/1991/07/26/obituaries/isaac-bashevis-singer-nobel-laureate-for-his-yiddish-stories-is-dead-at-87.html

Straus, E. W. (1966). *Phenomenological Psychology: The Selected Papers of E. W. Straus*. New York: Basic Books.

Trump, M. L. (2020). *Too Much and Never Enough: How My Family Created the World's Most Dangerous Man*. New York: Simon & Schuster.

Winnicott, D. W. (2016). *The Collected Works of D. W. Winnicott*. Ed. R. Ades. London: Oxford University Press.

Chapter 4

After the Election

Between Truth and Lies and More

The world is still in election ferment and longer-lasting ferment in general. Yesterday the electoral vote came through safely and clearly amidst turmoil, lies, fraud accusations and attempts to manipulate vote counts. We will have a new president, Joseph Biden, on January 20, 2021. To amplify Bion (1991, p. 41) there are conditions in which lies and truth can be indistinguishable. Lies masquerading as truth can stimulate strong autonomic responses that give the brain a sense of unity or are a kind of unity in profoundly convincing ways, often allied with an I'm/We're right-You're wrong rush of power. As Socrates pointed out, beliefs can substitute for truth and play injurious roles in wars of power. We have two more dates to go through on the way to a change in presidency, one of them on January 6 when all the crazies can happen.

Relationships between truth and lies are still evolving. Many variations are largely unknown and what we think we know can help or harm. Bion has amazing discussions of truth-lying. One of his statements, observations, fantasies is put in the mouth of the character called Robin in *A Memoir of the Future* (Bion, 1991, I: 11, p. 49): "Lies and Truth are indistinguishable!" Robin expresses hellish agony caught in an endless war with an unknown, nameless enemy. To postulate equivocation of "the fiend that lies like truth" pales in the face of deeper complexity, although it is bad enough. Fiction and reality blend, made of many kinds of blends.

Lies can be gateways to truths, like fiction. In a way, good fiction isn't a lie, it's attempting to portray aspects of emotional truth, what it feels like to be alive, what life itself is like. In giving expression to felt experience fiction is akin to myth, another form of storytelling. Making up images and stories to communicate emotional experience has many valences, with metaphor and analogy among its tools. So 'truth" can be a funny word made up of varied ingredients, including contraries and their spectrums, to the extent that what passes for truth can be a lie. Jesus called people hypocrites who appeared to be honest, devoted purveyors of religion. And when summoned to judge Jesus Pontius Pilate is said to have asked, "What is truth?" It is commonplace to say what is truth for one is falsehood for another but the matter can

DOI: 10.4324/9781032658926-5

be more serious and even deadly when in political life lies and truth reverse or fuse. We take for granted that propaganda uses truth in selective ways. One might almost say that lies have their truths and truths their lies. We speak of white lies mitigating cruel truths. Bion speaks of "truth compassion" and "truth cruelty," in which truth itself becomes demonic. In what ways can we speak of the good and/or evil that truth can mediate?

Some of you probably read or heard me say that possibly the first time I heard truth in a way that I totally believed it was Socrates, whom I met in my sophomore year of college, a decisive moment. He apparently allied truth with "the form of the Good," perhaps a cousin of "basic goodness" in Buddhism. One can hear echoes, in some aspects, of the biblical God as well, a good that runs through and permeates existence. Socrates emphasized self-knowledge (Bion's K) as a path. Saint Paul emphasizes love (Bion's L), "God is love." Although he also says," What a dreadful thing to fall into the hands of the living God." We haven't stopped – we might add P for Psyche, another gift from ancient Greece. Psychoanalysis posited, described and expressed ways aspects of psyche are projected into the world – so many links between inner-outer realities. One might caricature this by saying, "What's in is out, what's out is in." Such caricature can be part of dreadful-beatific realities. Bion depicted the horrors of war as a way to depict externalized aspects of our psyche, if only we could catch on. He spoke of nightmares and daymares.

Is there truth without language and, if so, what would that be like – or just be? So many writers use language to depict or express felt experience, feeling without words, or even feeling that has not been named before. Over and over Bion has his characters call each other fictions, imaginal fragments or moments, all of which give some expression to the truth of experience, the truth of life in one or another way. Myself (p. 124) speaks of "a mental digestive system" which fictions feed and aid, "… the mental diet of entertaining fictitious characters has contributed greatly to my mental health." It is often said that truth nourishes and lies poison and there are moments that applies. But it is also the case that emotional truth can nourish through fiction. Our relation to experience and sharing it is multifaceted and still growing.

Language creates lies and truths, takes away from the truths of being, adds to the truths of being, can create experience. Speaking tries to express and/or hide experience. One of my favorite examples is Rilke who seems to create experience as he writes. We live dialectical mixtures of capacities. Someone was telling me today he was trying to give expression to something he couldn't express, something he couldn't get to through language. And as he spoke the wordless experience became a felt presence. He or "it" somehow conveyed the unsayable and I could feel it, a shared moment of feeling what could not be said. There are times that feeling comes through dimensions we don't know we have.

I learned as a child that "little white lies" can smooth rough spots over and help move from moment to moment, from here to there. I marveled at the saying, "The truth can set you free." But as I grew became aware of horrifying situations in which truth can wound and injure. Truth can kill and lies can poison. Are we caught between evils, our power of discrimination so meager? It was a big thing in the Middle Ages to try to learn how to tell the difference between God and Satan, insofar as one could.

Bion spoke about the cruel use of truth and compassionate use, 'truth cruelty' and 'truth compassion.' In *Coming Through the Whirlwind* (1992) I wrote about a therapist who used knowledge of psychological truth not only to wound patients, family and friends but perhaps most deeply himself. It was as if he lived in a moment that said, "My perception of your lies is the truth." A moment that turned against himself as well. Often ways we use truth and lies wounds ourselves. As our work unfolded his keen, wounding perception became a vehicle for helpful caring as healing links grew between brain and heart.

Mycroft, Sherlock's older brother, begins a diatribe about the mind (1991; Book 1, Chapter 20, p. 95). Conan Doyle represents Mycroft as smarter than Sherlock. We know how clever Sherlock can be, an ace sleuth, solving crimes. We might say that Mycroft is an explorer and spokesperson for mind itself. I'm tempted to say he may appreciate and love the mind for its own sake, whatever its unsolvable qualities and mysteries. He makes it clear that the human mind most exercises him. He has no easy answers for what it is or how it works but thinks causal association with the central nervous system is insufficient. In that regard, he feels Freud's association of mind with anatomical processes is inadequate and recalls the belief in Ghosts by ancient Greeks. He asks what "visible counterpart" can "apprehend a personality after the physical anatomy had been destroyed or dealt with ..." They did not see "ghosts" with "the physical, sensuous, visual apparatus." What kind of seeing is this? Freud called our ego both a reality testing and hallucinatory organ. Mycroft seems to be more than hinting about some kind of extra-physiological dimension.

Can there be pure mind without a body, some kind or transcendent mind?

Mycroft seems to posit the immaterial mind while other characters present varied dimensions of mind-body possibilities, e.g., body-mind, sensation-mind, feeling-mind, intuitive-mind, degrees of embodiment and worldliness. With Mycroft the contrast between mind/body is extreme while other characters express different facets of mind-body spectrums. Mycroft adds the Greeks spoke about "phrenes" (mind) without settling or seeming to need a concrete physical apparatus, although some thought it was in the head or heart or guts, all of which played a role in language.

The history of body-mind functions and representations is long and complex. Hindu chakras, the Kabbalah Tree of Life (sephirot), Tantric Buddhism are among the systems uniting body areas and functions with psychological-mental processes. Kabbalah adds nameless divine dimensions beyond anything physical. Taoism also refers to nameless inner treasures and states with no specific location. We have residues of such ancient traditions in modern philosophy, e.g., Freud's body and mental ego, Husserl's empirical, psychological and transcendental ego, all with important arrays of capacities and functions.

Complexities pile upon complexities. Mycroft, who seems to affirm transcendent, immaterial mind and thought itself, has a name that refers to a small farm, my-croft. It is as if his mind is a farm of his own and, perhaps an inner farm with no material location, a mental farm of a certain kind, a thought farm. I might be tempted to think of Heidegger's Eigenwelt, worlds of one's own self, which Mycroft represents one part of. Or, perhaps, he is a part that transcends all parts, if that were possible.

Characters poking fun and adding-subtracting from each other runs through Bion's *A Memoir of the Future*. In some less violent ways, this happens with Mycroft and Sherlock too. Mycroft is mind itself for its own sake. His younger brother, Sherlock, is a version of a kind of practical mind, a particularly investigative practical mind seeking solutions to criminal acts. Can Sherlock dare Sherlock to find the cause of the crime of existence, the criminal acts we live by and often need for psychic and physical survival? Is Mycroft always a cut above and Sherlock a bit below? Younger Sherlock is beset with problems, including a cocaine addiction, something the father of psychoanalysis also indulged until one of his patients died from cocaine. He learned that the relief cocaine supplied from anxiety-depression could lead to permanent cure of non-being.

Somewhat fittingly, Mycroft died of a brain hemorrhage. Sherlock plunged to his death off a cliff locked in a struggle with his evil enemy Moriarty (a kind of hero in Beat literature). In a few years Sherlock was brought back to life because of public outcry and the struggle with evil continued, as it does for most of us.

Sherlock has received many diagnoses by readers, including tendencies such as Asperger's, manic-depressive, asexual, psychopathic. But he was an inveterate sleuth and his high IQ spiked curiosity, search, and cogent speculation. He had a strong quality of perseverance but suffered damage as well as relief from his addictive needs. Are there always or often ways one is one's worst enemy as well as sometimes friend?

Brother tales are ancient and tend to overshadow sister tales, although both are powerful expressions of inner-outer forces. Various divisions and variations of good-bad run through them. In Genesis, the first siblings result in murder, although the story does not end there, as though the stories twist and turn for centuries, indeed, millennia. Nor does Cain, the first biblical murderer turn out to be all bad. Killing his brother and earning God's protective mark opens paths of wandering and building. Competition so often lies in the background but also something more. Cain the farmer offered wheat from his harvest; Abel the shepherd a firstborn lamb. Apparently, God was not a vegetarian as he favored Abel's meat. Is it an accident that meat has eat in it? Yet through an act of murder Cain survived to continue life's journey while Abel's blood cried from the ground. We often say God works in strange ways, and to us it feels like cruelty is part of it.

One way psychoanalysis makes sense of this is to think of mythic brothers, twins, associates as different aspects of human personality, capacities, qualities, aspects of oneself. M. Klein speaks of a need for reparation and Cain in his search and growth became a builder of cities. The latter, I feel, is more than reparation, it is a development of one's being, one's person, one's gifts and use of them. A challenge of turning bad into good, murderous energy into productive building. I used to have a political science teacher who liked standing in front of class saying, "In order to build you must destroy." A variation of a saying I used to see on Con Edison signs when I was growing up. Making use of destructive energy and turning it into something good is a theme that runs through literature, thought and art, as, also its counterpart, spoiling of the good turning into destructive wounds. There are times murder is a short way from self-murder in its varied forms.

Ishmael-Isaac, Jacob-Esau, Joseph and his brothers ... Sarah-Hagar, Leah-Rachel, Martha-Mary ... add your own favorite twists and turns. Different parts of the psyche, different moods or elements of existence? An interweaving, mutating binary codified in the 19th century with Dr. Jekyll and Mr. Hyde. But then we already had the long-lasting binary God-Satan – twins? Enemies? Portrayals of attitudes, inclinations, needs, emotional and mental malignancy and potential. Who do you see in the inner mirror day to day, moment to moment? Who are you seeing now? We owe history and culture much in giving us a multitude of characters to draw from, still growing dramatis personae of our psyche. Complexities and nuances of self-creation are still developing. Sometimes the difficulties are too much and we try to solidify ourselves and hold on to simplified versions. In the external world, oversimplification can degenerate into literal wars instead of learning to work with wars-peace within. X vs. Y can form a basis for a field of experience that needs broadening and enriching, although it has its own creative moments as well.

One might think most insight into lying could come from studying psychopathy – those with a pronounced psychopathic personality and the psychopathic attitude or aspect of personality that is part of many if not all of us. But dedicated psychopathy may scarcely be aware of itself. One is used to lying to gain advantage or survive. One chronically lies about lying and takes for granted that's the way life is. He would be a fool otherwise. Such an organizing attitude may involve parents who cannot supply needed emotional nourishment and if the baby-child is going to get anything out of life it must get it himself any way it can. A quasi-predator attitude is evoked for sustenance. In psychosis realization that one is living a lie or that life is a lie is devastating. In some hopelessness is so intense that dying becomes the only truthful thing to do. There is no possibility to rid oneself of lies, so what's the sense of going on? There is no way out of the pervasive tyranny of Satan, Father of Lies. I once asked O. Hobart Mowrer if he could say something about the difference between psychopathy and psychosis. Mowrer spent time in mental hospitals as a patient. He started "truth groups" there. He looked at me kindly and answered, "Some people don't have the common decency to go crazy." It touches life's paradoxes to think of Mower in hospital and being a President of The American Psychological Association.

Many patients reach a point where they feel helpless facing the lies of life. Yet that point can be part of a transformative process. Moments of growth give birth to more moments of growth and we are born, partly giving birth to ourselves all life long. I remember a patient who had been hospitalized telling me he hadn't expected it to be so awful. I thought for a moment and couldn't help saying, "Yes it can be awful. I feel what you are going through. But like life awful is a funny word – as if some part of you is saying it is filled with awe." He was taken aback and thought a long time and then said, "How did you know my secret feeling? When I'm by myself and quiet and feel my soul beats I think yes, awe is deeper than the rip and hurt and wound I feel." "Both are there," I said. "Yes, both are there," he echoed. I felt we were sharing something deeper than the agony without lying about the latter, that the bare fact of deep experience opened the possibility of something more.

Another patient cried-screamed, "I'm shattering. Breaking. My insides are breaking into millions of pieces of sharp glass. My insides are broken glass, breaking and breaking and you can't see them, can you." "No," I say, "but I can feel you are being cut by your own insides." "Yes," he says, "my insides are cutting me and blood is … ." He pauses and I think of Bion's repeated phrase and say, "Blood everywhere." "Blood everywhere," he repeats. I think of the biblical phrase, "The soul is in the blood," and when he hears the phrase he looks at me intently and we are quiet for a long time. As he leaves the session he says, "The soul is in the blood."

There are ways in which being together is soul creation, soul discovery. I am touched by Rabbi Schneerson's remark that "God creates the world anew from nothing every moment." What these patients who felt hopeless begin to sense is that some sense of creation is part of being, their beings, a kind of regeneration process begins to grow. Once a person told me, "I throw myself against the wall every night and break like a bottle. But what I am doing here helps me feel the bits and pieces can be part of growing."

Another patient who found his way to my psychic playground after several hospitalizations said, "I read some of the passages in Bion you talked about – truth and lying becoming each other, the lying truth and truthful lie. At first I thought, 'How can this be? Truth is truth and lies are lies.' Then I wondered how it ever is otherwise.

"I remember my mother saying, yelling, cajoling, accusing, "You're lying to me!" Now so many years later I can feel the moment I was murdered. The moments I was murdered and this was one of them. Murder was in the room. Lying can lead to murder. Just the reverse of why you lie. You lie to avoid murder. But now I know things in ways I didn't then. One can kill oneself if one discovers one lives a lie, one's whole life has been a lie. Let me confess it and see how it feels right now with you. My whole life has been a lie. I am a living lie."

"All of your life," I ask. "All bits of it? Can you say there never was a moment of truth and beauty?"

"The truth is I'm a lie, a living lie. But you touch something important. Good things happen. And yes, there are moments of beauty."

"And Keats says ..."

"A thing of beauty is a joy forever," we both say together.

"I've been lying to myself all my life," he continues, "but bits of beauty break through, bits of beauty truth. Maybe beauty is a fiction too, some beauty – but there is beauty truth, too, real truth, real beauty."

"Yes," I feel and share. "And different ways of using truth, beauty, lies as well."

"You told me about Bion writing about 'truth compassion' and 'truth cruelty.' The cruel truth or cruel use of truth. The saving lie, at least for moments. How do we get out of this? As I say that a voice says, 'How do we get into it?'"

"I think we are very much in it in some way. In and out at the same time."

"This is a precious moment. You are touching me."

* * *

Later I thought again of Rebbe Schneerson speaking of God's continuous creation each moment. There are many ways this can happen. Many kinds of moments and many kinds of creation. Now I think of Ben in *Coming Through the Whirlwind*. Ben was a therapist who used therapy truth to hurt people and gain power over them, often imaginary power. In *Whirlwind* I document aspects of our years of work together in which he grew and became better. Better at lying, better at truth telling and better at being compassionate. He moved from a position of feeling, "My perception of your lies is the truth," to a more complex, multisided feeling of the depths and difficulties of the human condition. A caring rather than denigrating one-up sense of being with patients, family and friends.

Lying can alter reality and even create reality. Lying is part of reality and affects the way we see and change things. Cigarette and insecticide companies lied about the harmlessness of their products, emphasizing benefits. We face this quandary with energy products. It is an ancient coupling, harm and benefit, loss and gain. Poisons as well as knives and guns have changed reigns of power.

In a way, Mycroft takes us deeper than lies to varied visions of mind, mind thinking about itself, different uses, levels, dimensions of mind, embodied-disembodied mind, immanence-transcendence. If there is an error in thinking it cannot simply be equated with lying. Error and fallacy can be part of sincere thought. Being fallible is not identical to lying, although relationships between fallibility and self-deception may be complex and varied.

Mycroft (1991, p. 95) wonders what function enables people to imagine the existence of personality after the physical anatomy suffers destruction. What capacities are involved in apprehending a "personality"? Bion talks about a particular moment in evolution where interest in integrity, how one lives, with what quality, supplements and at times surpasses the drive for physical survival. How one survives as a *person*, a caring, growing being is added or even transcends the will to survive. *How* one survives grows in importance. In certain instances, integrity and survival may compete with each other for preeminence. What quality of survival? What quality of integrity?

There are so many stories, viewpoints, or as Bion might say, vertices, myths about mental life e.g., Hermetic philosophy in antiquity alive today. Pierre Teihard de Chardin, a Jesuit paleontologist, depicted an evolutionary path through geosphere, biosphere, noosphere and even further if one can imagine what he called an Omega Point, akin to the spiritual nameless dimension in Kabbalah touching Ein Sof. He was concerned to show the whole universe participating in the movement.

Even though Freud posited a neurological underpinning of mental functions he came to a point where neural understanding was insufficient when it came to imagining how psychic life works, including what one could consciously experience and unconscious processes accessed by conjecture. Now you can see brain waves on a screen and even correct certain neural malformations and malfunctions but be at a loss by the transformation of physiological work into experience. Even more so when experience pushes evolution, pressuring growth of physiology to support it. There may be leaps of thinking, philosophizing, experiencing, art and writing that the brain has to catch up with and develop circuitry to support the experiencing of a world that's on the way, a dialectical interweaving where one set of systems stimulates another, jumping ahead and catching up.

It may be what we call lying and truthing stimulate each other in myriad creative-destructive ways. Bion speaks of aspects of criminality that stimulate growth of knowledge and psychic evolution. At the same time, he speaks of the psyche's need for truth as the body needs physical nourishment. He has many depictions of war and catastrophic links as ways we bind together as well as tear ourselves apart. In a way, Myself tears ordinary experience apart although he values it immensely. He touches "opinions" that arise from subjective depths without claim to, as Shakespeare put it, "a local habitation and a name." He feels ineffable sensing or intuitions give rise to formless thought, ideas, opinions, fictions that are superior to those one can claim authorship or ownership of. He goes further and says these fictions, imaginings, opinions, beliefs have more value in "a war for supremacy" than "a statement with a vertex of truth value." (ibid., p. 95) In other words, lies can be better weapons than truth in "a struggle for supremacy." Motivation, attitude, goal, function has its own lie-truth grids.

"A struggle for supremacy" is one attitude. A peace that passes understanding another. 19th-century psychology depicted the struggle of ideas to be focused on by consciousness. There was not only a limen ideas had to pass in order to be noticed but had to elbow out other ideas to become a focus of conscious attention. Is there such a thing as unconscious attention and what would that look like? Freud depicted varying degrees and qualities of unconscious, preconscious and conscious content. The *Lankavatara Sutra* depicts unconscious states, depths and dimensions that can support the growth of Enlightenment. There are many writings that depict and express creative-destructive processes with varying depth and qualities. I suspect there are ways to write that can create such processes as well.

The competition of ideas for attention of consciousness gained a lot from Darwin's struggle for life and survival of the fittest. Even ideas have lives and developmental struggles, a sense we see working from cellular on. Freud's structural theory expressed a kind of struggle for supremacy of different structures and capacities. It also touches moments of harmony as well, so that struggle-harmony have many kinds of relationships and variations. A model of control has dominated much of world history. Control, opposition, fusion. Perhaps a partnership model would offer more avenues of co-nourishment. The likelihood is we are far from exhausting possible ways of apprehending and delineating ways things work and new kinds of processes may still be on near-distant horizons as well.

Body-mind processes take many forms and give rise to many kinds of experience. At times, the body can feel immaterial and mind material. Each may vanish into the other or disappear into itself. In the early Middle Ages, mystics spoke of the body as a prison but we can be prisoners of our mind as well. In psychosis mental products become terrifying, issuing destructive commands and taking horrifying forms. If we try to escape the so-called physical we may be trapped by the so-called immaterial. Body experience can be ineffable in delightful ways.

Phrases like "Pride goeth before the fall" echo through the ages and we are fascinated by the burning of our wings when we fly too close to the sun. Yet both falling-flying are part of our psychical beings, caricatured in manic-depressive movements. Is there a war for the possession of the psyche between truthing and lying? When I hear the kinds of lies psychopathically disseminated as truth in the political world I wonder what is true about psychopathy? It is a very real survivor orientation aimed at domination and evasion of domination. A destructive way to try to keep from being destroyed, a way of controlling fear of destruction. How can a lie be truth for 43 million people, a lie for 48 million? A lie for one is truth for another and truth for one is a lie for another. What kind of a psyche do we have? What is our makeup? We trick each other and ourselves. Animals get by with trickery too. When does tricking oneself help or harm and how?

Freud codifies ages of sophisticated perception of ways humans fool themselves and try to fool others. He delineates ways we defend ourselves by hiding from ourselves. We can call our defenses ways of lying, but they also aim to help us survive our selves and life. A version of the truth of lying and the lying truth is in Jodorowski's movie *El Topo*. The hero is on an enlightenment journey and must kill a master of the desert in order to survive and progress. A subtheme has to do with rigidity of perfection and creative fallibility. One encounter was a gun dual in which the master shot first. The hero, knowing the master's "perfection" had placed a smallish metal shield over his heart area under his clothes. The perfect shot knocked him down but after a few moments, he recovered and shot the master dead. I felt he almost gloated as he removed the shield and bullet in triumph but perhaps he simply was acknowledging the truth of the situation, it's not good to be too good. But on reflection, who was more perfect? His calculation of the master's power and response – didn't that have a kind of superior perfection of its own? Didn't the master prove to be even more fallible? What kind of beings are we and how do we work with ourselves? What kinds of metal plates do we have around or in our hearts and how do they function? So many heart shields for so many real or imaginary bullets – being tricky can have its value but almost any capacity can backfire. What role does fallible omniscience play in our lives?

And what would a mental plate around our heart look like? Philo-Sophia crossing the river or simply a cross? A war for possession that fits the current moment in a deep, spiritual way? A war for what kind of country and world we are going to have – can we have – a war for Dispossession? What kinds of lives will be lived (ouch – live has lie in it). What is the dynamic that flows through existence going to be and with what atmospheric quality? What quality of life?

Are there germs of integrity, germs of truth left in swirls of lies? At one moment Senator McConnell admits Biden won the election and Attorney General Barr resigns, as if keeping up the pretense became too much to bear. Another moment the lie is joined, as if confirming the character Myself's assertion that lies are more valuable than truth in wars for possession and supremacy (Bion, 1991, I:26 p, 95). In my online book *Age of Psychopathy* (2006) I write of psychopathic manipulation of psychotic anxieties, e.g., the

Bush administration justifying our invading Iraq by whipping up fears of Iraq's atomic weapons when no such weapons existed. They struck Iraq on their soil rather than waiting for Iraq to strike us, playing on annihilation and invasion dreads that went along with affirming and defending our own "identity" rather than submitting to theirs, something of a hallucinatory fantasy molding beliefs. At the moment I picture putting a sign inside ourselves: "Watch out! Watch out for your identity!" Better, multitude of identities. Don't be taken in by yourself. So much of what we think we are may be soaked by what Lacan calls imaginary rather than real. Too often we defend fictions at our own and others' expense.

One thing I love about Buddhism is it helps us slip through holes of our identities or between them. Treat your identities kindly but don't be taken in by them. They may have much to offer in building a life and culture but beware of what they may destroy. As with so many aspects of our makeup, handle with care in the ongoing dialogue of caution-recklessness. Each has so much to contribute but match gain with loss.

I think of sports games when I was a kid and moments where someone yelled (or screamed), "You're cheating," Could have been missing a base and saying you were safe, not crossing a goal line and saying you did, any number of ways evading loss and trying to win. There were little song ditties about losing-winning making fun of cheaters. Funny word with heat and eat in it. Even the word "out" has innuendos like "out of it," "outcast," "out of line," and any number of fears of being "out" and not "in" a group. And now cheating seems almost par for the course in political discourse and actions. Since childhood I've learned the importance yet fragility of law throughout ages, good laws, bad laws, fair and unfair laws. How to get it right and for whom? Talmud has significant discourses on details of age-old concern: how to administer justice justly. And now we have candidates running for political office promising to nullify or weaken internal and external judicial systems in the battle for supremacy.

"The truth shall set you free." (Jesus)_What is truth? (Pontius Pilate) Mommy lies to little baby, "It doesn't hurt." Make the hurt go away with little white lies and some big ones too. Truth frees. Truth kills. Lies poison. Lies salve. Truth is soul nourishment. Fiction is a form of truth. What will make me feel better? What helps you get into a better state? And what about forms of truth? God's voice of thunder, God's still quiet voice. Wrath and mercy, hate and love. Do you sometimes feel God screams like a baby crying to be heard?

Where does truth go when you're hiding? Is truth hiding with you? Esoteric literature is about hidden truth, a model Freud adopted, the truth of the hidden. There are moments when truth can't compete with lies. Can one tell the difference? In a way, what Freud called "defenses" are protective lies to blunt a sense of massive injury. Does personality have a truth antenna, truth attunement? Can truth make you President of the United States?

What kinds of power do truth-and-lies have? Can either stop death? What qualities do truthing-lying add to life?

What is truth for? What good is truth? What is it? You know you have to compromise some of your truths to make a living and get along with yourself and others. One might also call this a truth, another kind of truth. It's good to find a job you can function in, work that has truth in it, that has psychical value and meaning. Most of us here are therapists. Thank God we found a job that keeps us off the street and gives us some psychical work to do. In many cases the job found us. I had no idea I was going to be a therapist or all the ins and outs that led to it. Socrates was a fantastic therapist for me in my sophomore year of college, a kind of wake-up call that got through to me. Many threads, setbacks, awakenings and respect for crawling along as well. I grew up near woods and learned how important worms were for soil and food for others. Speed is not necessarily the most important thing in growth. "They also serve who only stand and wait." (John Milton) Creative waiting.

Participant: "You spoke about truth that kills and truth that nourishes. I remember Bion writing that the psyche needs truth as much as the body needs nourishment. I easily drop into confusion. Is "truth" real? Is real "true"? Many stories draw attention to things that have been secret and lied about. People coming into being by telling their stories, their truths or realities that were unappreciated or unknown or secret."

Mike: Complexities multiply. How does one use what happens in life? Complexity gets more complex. The stories one tells about oneself and about one's life, the *truths* of one's life can be used in a way that hurts you too. It depends, in part, how truth is handled: handle truth with care. There are passages Bion talks about the power of lies and how truth doesn't stand a chance. How do human beings build capacity for truth and ability to use it well? What would this capacity look like? One of the things he talked about till the end was building capacity to experience with particular emphasis on emotional complexity. To tolerate and work with experience rather than evacuate it.

One of Bion's avenues of approach was through literature. Literature, too, was a privileged psychic window for Freud. Bion also was a painter and approached expressive truth of life through art. History was important for him and he was a history major at Oxford before becoming a doctor. Francesca spoke about his love of nature and I think his ashes were scattered in a beloved area. I felt an instant rapport with Bion's love of Socrates. When I was a little boy it seemed that people used "truth" as a way to get me to behave in a certain way, "truth" as an exploitative, manipulative vehicle. When I was eighteen Socrates freed me from this degradation of truth in an instant one works with all life long. Toward the end of Bion's life the importance of beauty in psychoanalytic work gained emphasis, e.g., the beauty of an interpretation. He quoted Keats on the importance of tolerating and making creative use of ambiguity. Now I think, too, of Keats's "Beauty is truth, truth beauty …"

Participant:	Some of what Bion writes about lies sounds to me like Donald Trump, e.g., the power of lies in a war for supremacy. It's like he defines what truth is and his followers believe, a made up gospel that seems to make them feel stronger.
Mike:	Like the fiction that Covid is not very important to worry about or even that it's a hoax.
Participant:	Or that he won the election and that Biden is a false, fraudulent President. The democrats are cheating and the Maga are fighting for the truth. His group has created an alternative to truth they fiercely believe in.
Mike:	And maybe sprinkles of truth here and there make it even tastier and stronger. It's an intense moment but in one or another way it's been going on for many years. A recent opinion piece in the Times felt it began with Reagan. In a way that may be so but it reaches farther back, an ancient part of human nature. A difference today is modes of communication reaching worldwide instantaneously. In his own way, Reagan was a master of media, disseminating "information" often misleading taken as gospel. Not to mention "dirty tricks" like his people touring the Middle East saying not to release the American hostages till after the Reagan election. Carter seemed a media novice by comparison, a man whose thread of truth-goodness worked against his election. Hard to locate where or how or why it started but lying was already present in the Garden of Eden where the Father of Lies wreaked havoc with all too willing human allies. An "innocent" story documenting and heralding momentous consequences between the confusion and use of truth-deception. Both deception and truth have played a vital role in survival. Their mix-ups, oppositions, fusions and co-nourishment are ongoing.

In Chapter 20 (p. 95) the character Myself (partly a version of Bion's inner being) says, "… opinions expressed by me even if fiction are worthy of being treated with respect." The kinds of lies one tells and the kinds of fiction of one and one's identities may open avenues of deep truth.

A beautiful thing about language is it means so many things at once. A simple example of multi-directionality is Bion's use of "supremacy," who's going to rule over who and how, referring at once to internal as well as external war and struggle. What part of you is going to rule over you or other parts of you? At different times Bion has characters speak of a "war that never ends" and has another character ask, "Where is the war I won?" Psyche and society, to some extent, mirror each other while adding ingredients and diverging.

Pierre Janet would strike up conversations with delusions of a psychotic patient. "Tell me about yourself, tell us what you want," he might ask in an attempt to begin dialogue with an inner attacker. In psychosis and elsewhere, identity formations can take the form of commands. "I'd like to hear what you want from this man, what you want from me? You say do this, do that or meet with horror. Can you say how you got to be this way? Can you say something about your bio? What are you after? Do you know yourself? Tell us who you are or who you think you are."

We mentioned above that 19th-century psychologists spoke of the competition of ideas below the limen of consciousness competing for the attention of consciousness. A kind of sub-liminal sub-conscious area of mind where, in part idea formation, like dream formation, began a kind of battle for survival seeking conscious attention and development – a parallel background for Freud's depiction of unconscious processes. Myself emphasizes not only Interior (psychic) and exterior (environmental) Darwinian survival of ideas and territory, but "a struggle for supremacy" and "war for possession" in which truth has a lower value than whatever works to win. Could it be Myself considered being a fiction of higher value than the "actual" Bion, whom he called "a second class citizen"? Or perhaps he meant that the actual or even fictional Bion were not as valuable as the interior Bion ('Myself') who might also be a truth seeker.

This is followed by the character 'Bion" who spoke of Conan Doyle hating his characters (Holmes, Watson, Mycroft) for driving him off the stage, an author hating his characters for becoming more famous and interesting than himself. Bion also mentions Mr. Pooter, a late 19th-century fictional character (*Diary of a Nobody*) through which self-importance and taking oneself too seriously is explored and ridiculed. The character Bion goes on to ruefully say that Pooter and Watson remind him of his own self, his own interior being driving him off the stage of life like dreams do. (p. 95) The chapter ends with Sherlock and Myself opining that dreams are at the mercy of a dreamer and thoughts need to find a thinker. The author Bion presents us with hints and bits of processes that press for recognition and work as part of the challenge of being human.

So Bion and Watson get into a tangle. Bion was familiar with quantum work and entanglement. My little formula apes many similar ones: everything is one and not one at the same time. I began speaking of a distinction-union structure in *The Psychotic Core* (1986) and *Coming Through the Whirlwind* (1992). It is an ancient thought, one held together by what we might call a basic structure of paradoxical experience. H. Elkin (1992) links the infant's "smiling response" to a moment of bringing together the far mother, mother at a distance, and the near mother, the one that holds, touches, feeds. Near-far is a basic form of experience, like towards-away.

The competition of subliminal ideas to get attention reminds one of different parts of the self vying for room in the psyche or an infant's need for recognition – even a moment of being noticed and, of course, much more. There are amazing and horrible moments that can become frames of reference for other moments. On a somewhat later level, being left out or included can become a derivative development and, more intensely, feeling left out and included at the same time as an organizing affective background.

In some ways the whole of *A Memoir of the Future* is a kind of playground, grown-up baby Bion playing with multiple tendencies that don't get along together. The text as a psychic mirror raises the question: is getting along with yourself possible? Are you the writer of your own life? Who's writing your life and how? It is likely many writers are writing our lives and, also, ways we don't know who is writing our lives. In the Brazil lectures, Bion comments there is no Numero Uno. The idea of Number One is a fantasy, a delusion, a belief, a wish that human beings attempt to realize in all kinds of ways. I've spoken about a partnership rather than control model. Find ways of living a co-nourishment rather than dominance or war model, although in varied circumstances, all our tendencies and capacities can contribute to growth. How we live with ourselves remains an evolutionary challenge.

I think of my medieval history class in college with Dr. Seton telling us how the invasion of "barbarians" partly fertilized and energized Rome. In general, wars through the ages have been a source of cross-cultural nourishment as well as destructive. There were periods where it looked like mercantile travel and exchange could fulfill such a function but, tragically, it has not replaced war. Challenges of getting along with others and oneself remain, in some ways, more pressing than ever, notwithstanding the lessening of world poverty and increase in education and human rights. Aldous Huxley, worried about such difficulties, remarked that avenues for emotional education are sorely missing in our schools.

The character Rosemary asserts, "Money, morals, 'honours', position and power" are often used as counterfeit substitutes for real nourishment, buying the psyche off rather than fostering deep growth. Too often we practice "life *manque*" or as Wordsworth says, "Getting and spending we lay waste our powers." Rosemary adds the trenchant thought, "And now the mind has become available for the extension of lies, deceptions, evasions to produce bigger, better liars and cheats than any 'human' mind had so far achieved." (Ch 28, p. 129). Quite an achievement indeed.

And what about the present moment? A President of the U.S.A. who can't stop lying. An Attorney General who just quit as if reaching a limit to the lying capacity, at least for the moment. Attorney General Barr quit two days before this class apparently finding it too difficult to call Biden's election fraud. He helped two former presidents, Reagan and Bush, when possible treason charges might have loomed.

Participant: "Part of what he feared to repeat was the flowering of pardons that may be about to happen as happened near the end of the Bush presidency."

Mike: Perhaps he was just pushed a little more than he could bear. But he bore a lot. Lying about horrific causes doesn't seem to bother people, something noted in antiquity, for example, creating Satan as the "father of lies." Lady Macbeth's "Evil be my good," William Blake calls Satan energy and calls energy "divine delight." Alchemists tried to convert "shit into gold" and both Jung and Freud wrote about transformations of psychic energy converting bad into good or, to use Freud's quasi-alchemical formulation, creative sublimation (recalling ancient references having to do with converting base to sublime). Positive use of negative energy, creative destruction one such term, seems an important part of psychic work. Negative imagination has a lot of positive energy that keeps giving birth to ourselves There wouldn't have been a *Paradise Lost* without it or *Paradise Regained*. John Milton was all about loss and birth.

Participant: I hear you saying lying does not necessarily have the first or last word whatever its power at a certain moment of individual or group history. You talk about experience powering evolution and part of experience is our growing truth sense. One group may feel X is true and another that Y is true. They disagree about what is true but share a truth sense about their beliefs. Each has a passionate sense of truth that can ignite war or cooperation and even learning. Our system of government was meant to make room for many opinions in the expression and search for truth. Both sides feel passionate about what they believe is true.

Mike: Did Hitler believe Jews were poisoning the blood of Germany – was it true for him? In what ways is war truth? It has been said Western literature began with a war about an erotic theft (*The Iliad*). Freud depicts psychic conflicts and in some ways may also have an inner war image mind. Language speaks of being at war with oneself.

In this moment of history what kinds of truth wars are there and how do lies power them (and vice versa). On another level this moment may be helping us birth multiple perspectives that work better. A classic aporia: a Cretan declares all Cretans to be liars. An impossible moment, a moment of doubt can give birth to further dimensions and possibilities of experience, more to explore. Did you ever meet someone for whom truth is always a lie and lie takes the place of truth? H.L. Mencken predicted such a man would someday be president of our country, satisfying a perverse soul hunger. At the same time might it be possible to learn how to use lying-cheating abilities for good? People have known about this for a long time, giving expression to it in myths of negative creators where good becomes destructive and destructive becomes good. Freud spoke of reversal as earlier than repression. A word that has some vogue in popular culture is "meta" – above and beyond or in addition to, a view not saddled to binaries. It could also mean more to go. Learning to make a little better use of all our capacities. Negation has contributed a lot to human life and may have even more value the more we learn to use it well.

Cognition can take us to all kinds of places and we need it to build and survive. At the same time Bion values a kind of positive negation that takes us to a place of not knowing – an open place for the moment not filled or dominated by understanding or desire. Again, the challenge of multiple capacities and states learning to live together, not just against but with. In the Bible, God creates the world from nothing and chaos. A very valuable nothing and chaos, fertile tools of creation but also of value for their own sake. Creative nothing and chaos that gives us time off from our usual demanding identities. Bion uses the notation "O" as a signifier for the unknown-unknowable in a session. O might be omega or zero but also creative openness. He speaks of F in O, moments of faith as openings to the unknown, perhaps unknown emotional states awaiting birth and recognition. I've written (1992) that emotional states are embedded in attitudes and that work with emotional attitudes is crucial to find better solutions than actual physical war (inner creative war is another matter). Bion's F in O has also been likened to Buddha's *sunyata*, emptiness, a kind of inward creative emptiness opening new dimensions of being. The chapter "I Don't Know" in Contact With the Depths (2011) gives some history of "unknowing" as part of psychic fertility. A metaphor likening the swing of a pendulum stopping at each end of the swing to moments "between" states recalls an emphasis on "between" in Winnicott's work indebted to Buber's. "The unknown to the unknown" is one phrase representing a mystic's relationship with God. In psychoanalysis Matte-Blanco's (1975) "symmetrical unconscious" and in physics Bohm's "implicate order" connect with aspects of Bion's work (for more details see Chapter 1 in Contact With the Depths).

It sounds kind of odd calling "unknowing" a form of "knowing." Perhaps there is a way all experience is unknowing-knowing. But we keep on pushing deeper and deeper, as though attracted by indefinable-ineffable states as part of our beings. I think of a Hindu exercise I used to do as a young man but now seems to have became an unconscious habit more than sixty years later. Repeating "Who am I" "Who am I" looking at a mirror by candlelight in a darkened room as your face undergoes changes. One of my favorite radio shows (there was no TV) when I was a child was "Let's Pretend." In Midsummer Night's Dream Theseus says the poet "gives to airy nothing a local habitation and a name." Kabbalists seeking God burst through designations of YHVH (Yahveh) or Eyeh Asher Eyeh (I AM, I AM THAT I AM, I WILL BE THERE …) to Ein Sof – nameless Infinite. And yet many Jewish people when speaking of God use the word Hashem, the name. The name that cannot be said or pronounced or even known.

Bion repeatedly speaks of states and functions that resist definition and perhaps cannot be defined. Rosemary, who tends to function as a truthsayer and bringer down to earth character tells Bion "I don't know what you're talking about." One of the amazing things about A Memoir of the Future is that all the characters in their own ways function as truth purveyors. Truthsense runs through the book as an implicit "character." Even liars and cheats share in truthsense as part of humanity's makeup. Talmud points out sages may have opposite views but each carries a truth. Many-sided truth, reminiscent of Heraclitus's one as many, many as one.

The character Bion repeatedly says things like physical, sensuous experience and thoughts related to a thinker are in some ways definable. But "mind, personality, relationship, "belief" are not" (p 185). How does one move towards positive and/or negative ineffable states and further beyond +- valences. Bion's work dovetails with Husserl's failed attempt to mathematize consciousness and settling for becoming a "father of phenomenology."

I am this, I am that. "Tat Twam Asi"- You are that. That and What are "names" of the Nameless in Kabbalah, overlapping with Tao and emptiness – a living emptiness. God asks, "Where are you Adam?" Where has here in it. Here is a homonym with hear. One of Leonard Cohen's last songs has the Hebrew biblical word hineni in it – "Here I am, Lord. I'm ready." Reasonably defined, in some way you can define anything. Can you define yourself? Do you also elude definition? What does it mean to find your self? Or defy yourself? Literature, art. philosophy, medicine, neurology are going to be endless as long as our quest and need to express and learn and share continue. And its end-lessness is part of its challenging beauty – the privilege of being part of life's creation whatever ways you can. Yes, there are ways you can exhaust yourself but you still are part the inexhaustible.

Not all confinement is bad. W. Lowe, professor emeritus at the Candler School of Theology (Emory University) wrote about creativity spawned by limits, creative limits. God is said to have no limits – therefore, what kind of work can he do? What kind of work has no limits? One might say the limits of good creative work open infinity too. One might try to say all real literature opens to the infinite yet is based on emotional reality, fact, imaginal fact, truth that in its own way remains indefinable. Indefinable truth that makes life meaningful.

Bion speaks a lot about constant conjunctions (Hume) and counterparts – this goes with that. After all that, binaries, twins, siblings – mythic literature is filled with them. You can make up things that go together because they make up your experience: Sore – angry, hurt. Sore – Soar, Soar. Something else happens, something further, the ineffable happens. I learned about oscillating waves from the ocean as a child and later sound waves and waves of meaning. In all kinds of ways we never imagined we are still waving at and with each other. Who would have thought Shakespeare would have happened? Who would have thought Socrates would have happened? Who would have thought Freud would have happened? And Winnicott, Bion, or whoever, whatever opens reality. Reality keeps opening. Find what opens reality for you and keeps opening. Today is a sunny day in New York after many dark days. Bion quotes Saint John of the Cross and the dark night of the senses more than Freud in the beginning of his little book on *Caesura* ((1977). A dark night that opens reality. One might say Reality does not stop opening. But in the Hindu "trinity" Brahma is all, Vishnu preserves, Shiva destroys. So maybe I should revise my picture and say Reality keeps opening while it's here. May we all keep opening in our own special and shared ways while we're here.

I think of the Biblical Job losing everything (emptying out) and reaching a point where he meets God, a state where the Bible asks, "What did Job see too wonderful to know?" Or Winnicott's prayer, "Lord may I be alive when I die." Or Steve Jobs saying "Wow" in his last moments. Or Bion, in one of his last talks, speaking of psychoanalytic beauty. In his own way, through his own lifelong agony, love, appreciation and work, reality never stopped opening.

References

Bion, W. R. (1977). *Two Papers: The Grid and Caesura*. London: Routledge.

Bion, W. R. (1991). *A Memoir of the Future*. London: Routledge.

Eigen, M. (1992). *Coming Through the Whirlwind: Case Studies in Psychotherapy*. Asheville, North Carolina: Chiron Publications.

Eigen, M. (2006). *Age of Psychopathy*. http://www.psychoanalysis-and-therapy.com/human_nature/eigen/pref.html

Eigen, M. (2011). *Contact With the Depths*. London: Routledge.

Matte-Blanco, I. (1975). *The Unconscious as Infinite Sets: An Essay in Bi-logic*. London: Routledge.

Chapter 5

A Near Christmas Meeting

[Working with Chapter 6 "Shame" in *Image, Sense, Infinities and Everyday Life*]

We move in and out of many roles in our work, spontaneously, almost automatically moving from state to state depending on hosts of factors largely unconscious growing from psyche to psyche sensing and interaction. An extreme instance of this may occur when working with people who cannot feel themselves. Without quite realizing what is happening you may try to outdo them by not feeling yourself, forcing them to feel you not feeling them. In other words, they are forced to have a feeling in response to your lack or vacancy.

Some think of therapy as an art, particularly a form of drama, psychic drama. There are many contributors to this line of thought. One is Marie Coleman Nelson (1962). We met in 1974 when I took her continuous case seminar and remained good friends till her passing twenty-four years later. In 1985 we edited a book together, *Evil: Self and Culture*. As time went on I followed in her footsteps becoming, as she had, Editor of *The Psychoanalytic Review*. An aspect of her work I am thinking of is how a therapist spontaneously (and often thoughtfully) can enact different aspects of the patient's psyche, giving the latter a chance to express and work with reactive patterns that have been self-destructive. She called her work paradigmatic therapy, allied with field theory (1970). If the therapist occupies a part of the psychic field often occupied by a self-destructive aspect of the patient, the psyche is forced or pressured to reorganize to deal with the dramatized intrusion. More responsive rather than merely reactive possibilities begin to emerge. If you don't mind a bit of humor and take it with a grain of salt, if the therapist occupies the place of the patient, the latter has to regroup and find another way to be, in the long run more productive. Of course, this was only one of many possible interventions that could often take a creative turn. Marie was a closet poet deeply steeped in literary culture although she didn't finish college.

Nevertheless, one must be prepared for something going wrong, spiraling negative, vicious circles. One cannot be sure how the wheels will turn. Whatever it is, we try to work with it. Think of Andre Green's (1999) phrase, *the work of the negative*. And there are many moments when we are unable to tell what will turn out to be positive, negative or what kinds of mixtures.

DOI: 10.4324/9781032658926-6

As Marie aged she seemed to become more itinerant, moving from Manhattan to Long Island, then Kenya and ending up in Philadelphia. She also sold her summer house in Montauk, New York that we sometimes rented from her. She and her husband, the sociologist Benjamin Nelson, found ways of maintaining their marriage by living in different places and getting together when they could on weekends. Ben hired me to teach in a graduate psychoanalytic program at the New School, where I was working on my doctorate. His advice was, "Don't tell them everything you know. Little bits will be more than enough." When Marie moved to Long Island she started groups. She said that in Manhattan everyone was Hamlet but in Long Island you needed more people in the room to have a working psyche.

We therapists are a funny bunch but we're in there pitching.

Marie loved Kenya. She felt the people were honest. They matter of fact and kindly called her "old lady" because that's what they saw. She adopted a son there, a young man. When she came back she lived in Philadelphia and taught at the modern psychoanalytic institute until she passed away from emphysema at 82. I don't think she ever stopped smoking.

When it came to playing a role that was part of the patient's psyche, Marie tended to speak of playing a bad object in such a way that the person would see it in different ways and find new and freeing responses. In fact it is a gesture with a strong history, including Moreno's psychodrama, Fritz Perls' gestalt therapy, Joyce McDougall's theaters of the mind and body, and recently Lew Aron and Galit Atlas's portrayals of psychic drama. And remember, dramatic conflict was a basic theme in Freud, who was inspired by Sophocles to develop an Oedipus complex.

Participant: Is her field theory connected to Ferro's at all?

Mike: As you know, Ferro called his work a post-Bionian field theory. I'm not sure what post-Bion might be as field and quantum theories were inherent in Bion's work. One of Marie's emphases involved shifts of energy and affect in the psychic field. There is much overlap in the way different people use field theory, somewhat varied vertices, but they resonate with unknowable transformations in the *Lankavatara Sutra* and, in some sense, with Freud's depiction of reversal coming before and deeper than repression. Freud spoke of energy-affect shifts before set patterns get more rigidly organized. For example, in the Schreber case he portrays reversals of subject-object and affect (e.g., love-hate). One might add the play of opposites, turning against the self or other if "opposites" could be posited in the earlier shifts he wondered about. And "self" too can be other: e.g., Rimbaud's words, "I am an other." Existential writers depict ways we are both subject-object to and with ourselves.

If Freud had been born a little later he would have used field rather than post-Newtonian mechanical images and in many respects did so intuitively. One of my favorite quotes is Eddington's "Something unknown is doing we don't know what." How forces known and unknown work on each other from a distance is a common theme. If one is open to the unknown-unknowable one may sense intimations of dimensions with no name awaiting discovery and appreciation.

Bion's notation F in O offers some opening for the work of faith in relation to unknown-unknowable processes. Indeed, he called Faith the psychoanalytic attitude and by that opened a possible impossible field without memory, expectation, understanding or desire. Impossible, of course, but an Opening. One thinks of Buddhist sunyata (creative emptiness) or Marion Milner's 0 (Zero), perhaps even God's trembling over the waters in Genesis. Whatever it is or isn't that keeps opening possibilities. Part of Bion's emphasis was how to facilitate contact with unknown emotional experiences in sessions.

For some time in academic psychology there was a war between behaviorism's emphasis on cause-effect and gestalt psychology's emphasis on psychological, biological, physical fields characterized by spontaneous distribution of the parts, inherent processes made up of force fields in a particular group. Two of many examples given of the latter are the solar system and circulation of blood, spontaneously evolving organizations of interacting processes.

There are a number of ways of approaching field theories and they are still developing today. None are sufficient. In a way, nothing we do is sufficient. But so many factors contribute to how we experience experience. Some groups feel the whole universe is mental or has a mental component. Since antiquity and probably before, thinkers have been categorizing different domains of experience and temperaments. Closer to our time the Jesuit paleontologist, Teilhard de Chardin (1964) posited a developmental scheme moving from the physical (geosphere) to the biological (biosphere) to the psychological (psychosphere) to the spiritual (noosphere), all interactive and potentially co-nourishing. In a way, one must say mental life is inherent in matter or it could not have developed and continue developing. To make it a little more dramatic, some kind of mental life or potential is inherent in the very particles of matter, particles that make everything up. If not, how would any of this be here?

So how does any of this apply to Shame? I'm thinking of shambles (sham as related to shame and lying) and conflicts worldwide today. A famous quote from John Adams stresses the importance of morality for democracy to be possible: "Our Constitution was made only for a moral and religious People. It is wholly inadequate to the government of any other." Today lies are believed to be truths and people fight over the truth and falsehood of lies. As Pontius Pilate said, "What is truth?" Are we living now in something of

A Shameless Age? John Adams would not be surprised although he may have hoped for better.

And yet there are ways that shame does survive, including moral shame. I was reading that Abigail Disney felt that her uncle and father, Disney founders, would be ashamed of the way CEOs were treating workers now, especially during the pandemic. Not that Walt Disney didn't have his prejudices. But Abigail felt the gap between higher-lower is even greater now with more severe consequences, people not having enough funds or health care to get by. There is also more unemployment. Her latest film, critical of the Disney humanistic landscape, is called *The American Dream and Other Fairy Tales*.

Apparently, some part of this problem is occurring in my office building now. Not enough money is coming in to support the staff in ways they were used to. There is a possibility that more of the help would have to be let go. There is an appeal to the residents to make up the deficit and help out. I don't see how shame enters this as there is an ambience of shared attention, but it does mirror an economic travail the pandemic brings for some. Yet in the world today there is a lot of economic shame, humiliation and anger. It appears that this has been with us in one form or another for a long time. One finds examples of it in the Bible.

A lovely interview of left-wing evangelical Jim Wallace by Nicholas Kristoff in the New York Times (December 22, 2020) brought out good work related to biblical references. The Christian left has been overshadowed in the news by the Christian right as though a kind of civil war runs through many facets of our society and world. When Wallace talks about Red he means the red print used in certain New Testament Bibles when Jesus speaks. We can never know his exact words or even if an author is making it up but red print is used instead of quotation marks when Jesus is talking. Wallace points out that Jesus calls the priests "hypocrites": they confuse God with their own ego and celebrate the latter. In essence, Jesus tells Caesar to help people who need help, be good to the poor. He speaks for basic goodness, less vanity, although the two are often mixed in myriad ways.

There are two possibly three Marys who play roles in Jesus's life stories. His mother, the Virgin Mary, conceived him through the Holy Spirit. Mary an adulteress or prostitute who Jesus saved from stoning with the words, "He without sin among you cast the first stone." He supported her, too, with the words "She loved much." And the sisters Martha and Mary, the former caring for house and dinner chores while Mary sat at Jesus's feet listening to him. Jesus loved them both but defended Mary not helping Martha with the thought that Mary was attending to the Spirit, the one good part that could not be taken away. In the latter two stories, he seemed to defend the one attacked, a kind of reversal of values and meaning, as when he said the last shall be first. Scholarly and popular versions of these stories can differ, the latter blending the latter two Marys in various ways.

Jim Wallace might ask, "Where are the Christians today?" Or urge, "Read the red print in the Bible." The Christian left Wallace represents deserves more attention and support. You can Google him and his interview with Kristoff and see if it touches some good chords. Another reverend on the public scene doing much good or what good he can is James Clyburn (another Jim), a congressman from South Carolina. One way he is trying to make a difference is through caring legislation, where love and care have a practical say. It may be my prejudice but it seems to me hate plays a larger role on the Christian right. A split in the body politic, or perhaps some would say a split in the news and public media.

Perhaps the three (or two or four or more) Marys represent aspects of different human attitudes, modes of experiencing. Freud wrote about the importance of moods, nuclei of different states of being, moments. How may this apply to us in the service-help vocation? Are there ways we are psychic virgins, always beginning, opening, learning to touch and work with new domains of experience? Are we also psychic prostitutes, who emotionally dream with people in need of pay? And what about kneeling at the feet of the Holy Spirit, following its turns, letting it find us as we find others? Pure of heart, wily-innocent, knowing-unknowing, dealing with psychic evacuation and finding jewels.

When I was growing up I did a lot of diapering of my younger siblings because cleaning feces and diapering was something my mother did not like to do. In a way, have I found a profession where I can keep on changing my diapers as well as cleaning others and helping others to clean themselves? Freud associated an experience of evacuation with creativity and giving. There was a period after college when I used to clean toilets at Bickford's in Flushing, Long Island (flushing is an accidentally meaningful word here). A turning point came on Christmas Eve. I cleaned up, spudded potatoes, got everything ready for morning stragglers and took a break between shifts. I found my way to a nearby church and fell asleep in a pew. When I woke up mass was in progress and people carefully stood on either side of my sleeping body. Should I say my sleeping soul for I was deeply touched and began to weep. Within several weeks I found a job teaching fifth grade in a Bronx yeshiva and have been teaching ever since. Teaching is a form of learning, of course, and vice versa. Perhaps also a form of penance and something deeper as well, much deeper.

I wasn't aware of shame at Bickford's although some might regard cleaning toilets and vomit on New Year's Eve shameful. And yet I wept in church on Christmas. What kind of shame might Jim Wallace feel as a part of holy work? I picture him feeling that right-wing evangelicals were shameless in treating lies as truth. So many people doing so many things but splits run through them. And Abigail Disney picturing the shame her forbears might feel if they saw what was happening now – what kind of shame then, what kind now? And what kind of shame might Jesus mean?

I can't help slipping into a link between Shem and shame. A Jewish "name" for God is HaShem, which means The Name, standing for the Tetragrammaton one dare not pronounce. I wonder if Jung felt some kind of shame dreaming about God in Heaven on a Toilet Throne shitting on His creation. Or was it an act of defiance, ridicule and some kind of throwback to a two-year-old king on a throne. What kinds of wishes might Freud think such a dream tried to fulfill? Did it reflect a tension, at once all-powerful and powerless? One could go on imagining. I think to many now, this moment, it feels like God is shitting on the world, on us. Does God have different kinds of shame?

I wrote about how shame, guilt and fear have wounded my life (2016, p. 70). At the same time they added to my life, in some ways saved me from myself. A double-edged trinity, part of growth and/or pathology depending on how they function in a particular situation. At the moment, we have the pathology of too little shame and guilt in high places (e.g., Trump, Putin and groups and forces they represent). This is by no means so unusual. We call too little shame inhuman or associate it with psychopathy and certain kinds of narcissism. On the other hand, too much shame can be inhibitory, even paralyzing.

There are so many ways to turn against oneself to save oneself. French workers call attention to an "operational personality," trading feeling for functioning. People in high places may have lost the capacity to feel important emotional spectrums as a price for becoming keen "operators." Or it may be capacity to function saved them from an emotional life that was unbearable, a way of rising above deep pain.

Notions of building up and breaking down have been around a long time. Freud recycled these tendencies in his psychology as life and death drives, building unities and falling apart of unities. Some related terms in sciences are anabolic-catabolic, negentropy – entropy. I have heard people substitute diabolic for catabolic to give a sense of the building and ripping apart of meaning, so much so that lack of meaning and meaningless have become psycho-affective terms that describe aspects of experience.

Perhaps on an even deeper level, a perverse and negative version of Jesus's losing yourself to find yourself has to do with not being as a means of saving what one can of oneself. Here it is saving not finding. Many have voiced the sentiment that life isn't about finding oneself it's about creating oneself. At times negative destruction of self creates openings for self-creation. Whatever the variation, tone, and outcome, undoing self plays a very real role in life. Freud formulated this as a double tendency in a number of ways, e.g., turning against the self as a way to survive, doing-undoing and life drive-death drive. How difficult it is to understand, live with, transcend and transform self-hate as a survival mechanism to part of life's creativity. When Harold Bloom (1999) talked about Shakespeare inventing the human he may have had in mind inclusion of not being, e.g., Hamlet, "To be or not to be."

We are, of course, both. I am and am not in different ways at the same time. In both deep and surface ways, Hamlet expressed a simultaneity and juxtaposition of self-hate and self-affirmation.

When Bion spoke in New York (1977) the only analyst he mentioned from this area was Theodore Reik, his writings "On Surprise." I sometimes would think of inner surprise akin to a surprise party, "Surprise, Surprise," cheerfully echoed by inner guests waiting to be known, noticed, felt, appreciated, worked with, something like the song, "Hail, Hail – The Gang's all Here." An appreciative sense and openness to the unknown plays an important role in their work.

There are a number of other vocabulary confluences they share, e.g. their use of "dread" – Bion's nameless dread and Reik's depictions of trauma dread. There are moments Bion feels a sense of catastrophe links personality together as it breaks apart. Reik also emphasizes the power and work of catastrophic dread. One of the most important areas of his writing is the masochistic spectrum, from forms of self-punishment, self-hate, to something more formless, darker. I wonder what it would have been like if these men had met. Would they have enriched each other? Liked each other? Something more complicated? It might be fun to write an imaginary conversation between them, or a series of conversations. Reik was almost ten years older, one of Freud's earliest students, whom Freud helped out financially.

Both Reik and Bion had their share of professional ins and outs. Reik came to the United States at the age of fifty seeking refuge from the Nazis in 1938, the year Freud migrated to England at the age of eighty-two and died a year later. Reik discovered that although he was part of Freud's early group in Vienna the psychoanalytic society in New York would not give him full acceptance because he was not a medical doctor. He received a PhD in Europe for a psychology thesis on Flaubert's *Temptations of Saint Anthony* in 1912. He also had difficulties practicing without a medical degree in Europe and in defense Freud wrote *The Question of Lay Analysis* (1926). A perhaps unexpected result was that a learning group gathered around Reik in New York and gave birth to the first non-medical psychoanalytic institute, a movement that grew with much success, helping many.

Bion moved to Los Angeles in 1968 at the age of seventy-one. After Melanie Klein's death in 1960 deep dimensions of his creativity blossomed and four great works written (1962, 1963, 1965, 1970) caused mixed reactions, enough to make difficulties sustaining a practice, even though he was President of the British Society for three years (1962–1965). Things were not without problems in Los Angeles where the psychoanalytic institute would not grant him full membership. On Planet Earth these kinds of things seem to be par for the course, a President of the British Psychoanalytic Society not being accepted as a member of the Los Angeles

Psychoanalytic Society. In London he was felt to be not Kleinian enough, too mystical, perhaps even senile. In Los Angeles he was thought to be too Kleinian.

All kinds of divisiveness seem part of our makeup, as well as calls for harmony. Enough members of the Los Angeles society went into therapy or supervision and referred patients to him to help make his last decade in life fruitful.

One of the themes Bion and Reik share has to do with nullifying oneself in some way. For the moment I'll call it self-negation but it can work with multiple spectrums many ways. Bion speaks of plus and minus uses of capacities, e.g., +L, +H or +K and –L, –H, or –K, positive and negative functions of love, hate and knowing. One might speak of plus/minus kinds of nullification as well. A positive version is Jesus's losing oneself to find oneself or Buddha's creative emptiness that makes room for experience. A moderately negative example that Reik gives is hitting one's head by accident when closing the trunk of a car after packing to go on a trip, harming oneself to allay unconscious guilt, self punishment that gives permission.

Reik wrote a lot about what he called masochism, adding to a term Freud used, e.g., self-injury, expressing or placating a death wish or destructive drive. Following Freud, he saw psychic acts as blends between life and death forces that manifest in myriad ways.

Masochism often refers to taking pleasure in hurting oneself. It can also be a window on powerful and often fearful work of aggression turned against oneself, including various forms of self-hatred. There are many ways to hurt oneself besides obvious, seemingly deliberate self-injury. Falling down, biting one's tongue, lips, mouth, walking into a tree or moving car, ruining relationships as a form of self-protection-punishment, self-injury as a form of expiation, the list goes on. Shame, guilt, dread and anger can be ways of turning against oneself to mollify and appease a more relentless inner demand or pressure.

Beyond substituting pleasure for pain or pain for pleasure is a kind of zeroing out of personality, canceling oneself, ghastly loss of feeling, severe versions of depersonalization, loss of self. Bion describes catastrophic nullification of self, personality, feeling and speaks of "a destructive force that keeps on working *after* it has *destroyed* existence, time, and space," including destruction of anxiety and emptiness. One is left, in a way, to live without oneself. Therapy with a person who is not there must reach very deep places.

In a way working with ordinary masochism can be easier. One strikes a kind of masochistic balance, hurting oneself enough to go on living without killing oneself and even have some masochistic satisfaction in aspects of one's psychic wounds. Can we really know where or when a feeling of being wounded begins? Birth, pre-birth, post-birth – how does a primal sense of being wounded begin? Is it simply part of existence? We learn to work with it, modulate it and discover the mystery of deepening. The pain of life has been given expression since antiquity and before.

Part of the novel in art is the ways pain, pleasure, joy, suffering are expressed.

Our relationship to our wounds has so many aspects. Hurting oneself can even be an avenue of self-knowledge. In some cases, the pleasure of wounding myself is a way of letting myself know the wound is there. Is it possible to be wounded and not bother with it or know it is there? Look at a recent wounded president wounding, humiliating others. Wounding the whole society. He makes fun of people, wound causing wound, making others feel the wound that never heals and is out of reach. Maybe we can begin to catch on that when we do something bad to ourselves we might try to practice noticing an inner wound that wants a hearing. I think the whole of humanity shares deep inner wounds it hides and throws around.

What is the hidden wound? Shame, fear and guilt can be signals of processes, internal happenings and experiences we cannot tolerate and lack capacity to work with. Psychoanalysis and other therapies are some attempt to say yes, deep wounds exist, let's see if we can do something about them. We are not going to end being wounded. Wounding processes do not go away. But we may get better at working with them, better at relating, digesting, being with them in better ways – a basic human challenge.

I recently saw someone who said he lost all feeling four years ago. He felt he was just watching the world burn. He anesthetized himself as a way of getting through things but it was no solution. It was not enough.

Participant: What do you think of the idea of masochism being a kind of addictive excitement?

Mike: Phenomena that we call masochistic can take many forms, including what you are calling addictive excitement.

Participant: I feel in our country (U.S.A.), there is a widespread tendency to substitute excitement for something more meaningful. Excitement may satisfy, divert or relieve for a time but leave a deeper hunger, a deeper hole.

Mike: Yes, one can zero oneself out and not know it or partly not know it. In traditional literature, masochism is paired with sadism, a double tendency or two sides of a coin. I've heard it said that masochism is hidden sadism and sadism is hidden masochism. In some cases, there is excitement that can't be dealt with, e.g., free-floating, overwhelming excitement using masochism as a container or release. Instead of excitement that can't be dealt with, one talks about troubles and bad things that happened, a kind of chronic complaining. You are calling attention to widespread addictive masochistic excitement mistaken for real emotional nourishment.

I think you are saying something about the Trump era, where part of the psychology of the masses is a kind of masochistic excitement linked with Trump's brand of grandiose name calling, show of superiority, grievance, and humiliation as tools.

If one combines Balint's (1959) writings on thrills and regressions with Reik's 1939, 1941) on masochism one gets a plethora of combinations of dependency-superiority, exciting self-injury, blame-shame, feeling above instead of below. High-low often play important roles in masochistic excitement. There can be a perverse sense of superiority in masochistic submission, even trickery. A patient once said, "You want to know a secret? Something I feel like saying, 'Look at me. No weapons. You wouldn't want to hurt me would you?' It's a kind of feint like a boxer in the ring, outsmarting the dumb strong one. My weakness is stronger than your strength." He went on to speak of the power of cleverness, guile, a power in being weak. His description made me think of animals who play dead as a form of self-protection. Playing weak to avoid annihilation. Except in human life we really can deaden ourselves, nullify our psyche to avoid pains and torments. For some becoming alive again is a lifelong quest.

Spotnitz (1968) has an important variation on this theme: suppressing oneself to protect the other. Nulling oneself rather than the other enables one to survive – one needs the other for protection, help, nourishment from the beginning of life. Without the (m)other one would not, could not live. One turns one's murderous impulses against oneself to ensure the survival of the other and, in this case, oneself. Does this mean, in extremis, one may kill oneself to save oneself? When I was a child during World War Two, I heard of enemy soldiers killing themselves to save their honor. I also heard of people killing others as a form of self-protection. Reversals are a basic part of psychic operations as well as rigid organizations. As a psychologist I've grown in appreciation of seemingly endless melding and opposition of psychic tendencies and their shifting functions.

Participant: This weekend somebody sent me an interesting paper about grievances. Apparently there is research indicating that grievance lights up the same part of the brain as any other addiction. I thought of Trump's addiction to grievances that you spoke about.

Mike: Yes, so many ins and outs. At the moment I'm thinking of Edmund Bergler's work on injustice collecting, a chronic state or attitude of grievance associated with deep and early masochism. Magnifying and blaming others for all kinds of life's injustices can go along with a sense of moral superiority, better than thou, at times heightened unconscious megalomania which can justify horrendous acts. I would not be surprised to learn that some of the mass murders by young people today, detailed by our media, may have a thread of self-justification through injustice collecting, righting the wrong, imaginary or real, becoming superior to the injury. Or showing how damaged one is as a way of denigrating the other. Trump is not an actual killer but intensifies violent splits in the body politic that lead to societal damage. Yet many feel he makes the world better by humiliating the humiliators. Humiliation runs deep in our country as does getting back at. Both sectors in the personality are widespread. Masochistic excitement and thrill linked with narcissistic degradation and grandiosity help organize and stoke one's sense of grievance.

Addiction to injustice collecting and thrills one gets from blaming-shaming becomes a way of life. In *Emotional Storm* (2005, Chapter 10) I write about the use of shame and blame as cause-fillers. That is, instead of open waiting on the unknown or investigating complexities, shaming-blaming become easy substitutes for exploration. It's your fault-my fault take the place of discovery. We speak of the thrill of discovery but there is also a kind of gratification in blaming-shaming, even if it constricts the psychic field. "You're the reason why" or "I'm the reason why" pinpoints bits of annoyance and grievance that can be helpful if it does not foreclose larger possibilities.

Shame is more complex and has more tributaries than ordinarily imagined. Peter (2015, p. 72) talks about a closed door. He is talking about himself, a closed door within, a closed door in life. A few days later he says he can't keep up with himself, he's ahead of or behind himself. He disappears and wonders where he goes when he disappears. Shame makes him invisible and hyper-visible. Peter depicts shame, too, as a mouse that goes and goes and vanishes in an invisible hole.

Freud wrote about a tendency not to be, a kind of entropy of the self, a falling apart of unities. In physical terms, a gravitational pull in which organic dissolves into inorganic matter and personality moves toward zero, nothingness, if peace then a peace with no consciousness or animation. It can be difficult to find a balance between too much-too little aliveness in a particular situation. In *Psychic Deadness* (1996) I write about therapists being too alive or dead for a particular patient. In Chapter 15 "Being Too Good" I describe a therapist addicted to "perfection" who had to work hard to be a human being with her patient. Some patients can't take too much life and have to grow to let in more experience a little at a time. Freud wrote about flooding as a primal trauma – too much stimulation, more than the psycho-organism can handle. Through time, practice and growth, capacity develops to sense the emotional intensity a moment calls for. How much life can you take at a particular moment, or the next and the next? And what kind of life with what quality? There are so many ways to be attuned and/or misattuned.

I've worked with people who idealized the idea of rebirth or re-creation, wiping out the old with birth of the new. There certainly can be such moments in positive, life-giving ways. But more often being born again is a process over time and takes work. We can have rebirth fantasies that have value. But too often rebirth fantasies substitute for the actual process. We work with setbacks and little bits of growth, mixtures of mystery, practice, discovery and fortuitous moments that add to our repertoire of feeling. A patient said, "Yesterday when I was going shopping I saw a bunch of leaves on the ground each having five points. I couldn't believe what I was seeing and picked up a number and counted one by one. Five points each. When I first saw them I thought they were little menorahs – but that has nine candleholders. Then I thought of the stars on the American flag. Did they get the idea from leaves? When I saw the leaves I felt that fall was coming – fall was here. Such a beautiful season even with leaves falling to the ground, especially with leaves falling to the ground and the changing mixture of colors. When I raised my head I could see the sky through the tree branches, an open feeling. Life opening. I felt life opens little by little – sometimes it seems all at once. But over time, little by little with bigger and smaller moments, and I thought – that's like me, a good model for me. A bit at a time, all at once, and a little more. I felt myself breathing, no rush, in-out like the flowing of – well, time – here I am, 35 and appreciating the waving leaves."

At the time I felt he was having a Zen moment and in my mind and body saw and felt the waving leaves too. Almost as if our psyche is waving to us saying, "Wave to me too."

There are many ways to be reborn. In Chapter 2 of *Coming Through the Whirlwind* (1992) I bring out several. One can be reborn as a monster, a horror, as well as a more developed positive presence. Too often rebirth on the evangelical far right seems more a force of darkness than light, stripping away sensed complexity resulting in over simplified and sometimes dangerous attitudes, wiping out as much as it gives.

No group has a monopoly on madness. A kind of "rebirth" experience can make one feel right in some basic way. A "false rebirth" can act as a defense against the mess of one's makeup and twist one more out of shape, defending dogmatic "truth" that leaves little room for multiple viewpoints. Ironically, twisting oneself out of shape and narrowing one's mental-emotional field can make one feel more alive and ward off a sense of deeper deadness. The theme of deadness increasingly made its way into literature after the First and Second World Wars, e.g., T. S. Eliot, Camus and many others. Writings on psychic deadness spread in psychoanalytic work with difficulties related to not feeling real and alive (e.g., Fairbairn, Klein,

Winnicott, Bion and many more). What can one do in the face of an inner destructive force that continues after destroying "existence, time and space"? (Bion, 1965 p. 101) Can "false rebirth" be a way of protecting or diverting us from inner death? How often is suicide a way of escaping harrowing living death?

As touched upon above (p. 15) excitement may be used as an "antidote" for deadness but may lack the deeper nourishment personality needs. How does one distinguish between excitement and nourishment when there is so much overlap? Fairbairn (1966) tried to face this by distinguishing between exciting and good objects. He paired an exciting with a rejecting object under the heading "bad object," e.g., cycles of excitement-rejection. The good object is associated with real nourishment, affirmation and personal growth.

Of course, excitement and rejection can play a role in growth too. Fairbairn's way of handling this is to emphasize divide and conquer operations of the central ego, learning how to master conflicts such tendencies undergo. This leaves open what excitement and rejecting tendencies actually can contribute to personality growth, a subject of much exploration in psycho-analytic literature. Andre Green (1999) for example explores ways negative tendencies can add to personality, a theme basic in Freud's work as well. Prior to psychoanalysis William Blake (1790) called Satan Energy and Energy Eternal Delight, while Jesus mediated poetic Imagination, a kind of precursor of Freud's id and ego, a coupling with a long history.

An interesting side to Fairbairn's theory is that only the bad object is internalized, the good object doesn't have to be. One might get addicted to exciting or rejecting objects or cycles of excitement-rejection, or even the two fused and barely distinguishable. Perhaps Fairbairn is saying that the bad object needs to be represented in order to be worked with but there is no need to internalize the good object as it isn't painful or destructive. One needs to represent how one screws oneself up in life in order to work with it but the good object isn't represented because there's no need to represent it. It just is, offering good feelings. For Saint Paul Grace has no location, not his body or mind yet a wordless "place" he lives in that supports life.

I feel Fairbairn's description adds because it touches certain moments. But Melanie Klein depicts ways internalized good feeling offsets bad. Inner good feeling has a lot of work to do. Religions and spiritual paths, for example Buddhism, often affirm a basic goodness, which I'm tempted to call "primary goodness." But I've worked with people who feel there is no such thing as basic goodness or even feel that goodness is bad. Someone might say, "I am bad but goodness is deeper." But one also might say, "Each time I think I'm experiencing goodness I find I'm fooling myself and it's hiding deeper badness." In such moments goodness may feel hypocrit-ical, a pervasive lie.

To some extent, antiquity often linked evil with ignorance. Saint Paul seemed to disagree – he felt even when he knew what was good he did bad, the latter had a force of its own. Early Catholic authors also wrote of evil as an absence of good, a lack or privation. Since good is not defined as absence of evil it is a more primary state. Yet if one thinks of evil as lack of goodness it sounds pretty bad in itself. Throughout history both good and evil have been viewed as tendencies, capacities, actions, intentions, forces. We've tried to come up with all kinds of ways to speak about and explain why we feel, think and act as we do and jimmy it around to fit various functions and contexts. We have all kinds of ins and outs or, as Wittgenstein says, "nooks and crannies" and have been talking about them for thousands of years. With some luck we will continue experiencing and talking about our beings and makeup for many thousands more – and who knows what possibilities of growth lie ahead.

What can we say about the power of lies? Trump and many of his colleagues are still trying to steal the election. Are there moments when lies are more powerful than truth, infuse truth, inflate or deflate truth? Something about the emotional systems at work in lies seemingly give them muscle power, so that might, real or imaginary, makes right. As Socrates pointed out, beliefs are often taken as truth and have their own power. It may be part of why Trump's brother killed himself had to do with being unable to falsify himself enough to live the life his father wanted, while Trump outdid his father by becoming even more successful at his father's game. At the same time, one of Trump's streaks has to do with winning by losing. To put it oddly, making money by going bankrupt in limited ways, finding ways to turn loss into making money and wield a certain power. I'm afraid part of our country and our world is unconsciously suicidal in what I hope are limited ways. At times I wonder if something in him evokes a suicidal tendency in others masked as "righteousness." It may be important to pay attention to what can be "right" about lying as well as "wrong" about truthing. I think of Plato's distrust of the lies of poets while poets convey aesthetic and emotional truth. Is it possible that part of the world is committing suicide and part of the world isn't, like Freud positing such double tendencies within our personalities? The Bible, too, ends wondering which tendency will win, good or evil?

Since antiquity, faced with unsolvable knots of tendencies within and between ourselves, a sense, feeling, idea of rebirth or starting anew in a better way or higher level has been part of what we call wisdom literature. Freud writing to Fliess likened psychoanalysis to the ancient mystery cults concerned with psycho-spiritual transformation and rebirth processes. And here we are, Christmas days away, a messianic story of birth, death, resurrection in the face of inner-outer difficulties that appear to lack solution, a perennial birth that springs anew.

I'm afraid of the destructive tendency and I'm optimistic too. If part of the psyche and psyche of the world is committing suicide, another part is trying to save it. Thank God this week the internal Divine Messiah is going to be born [this talk was given two days before Christmas eve]. Let there be a little messianic birth in your life. A tiny particle, a tiny messianic birth, a little baby. All religious and spiritual paths I know emphasize some kind of psycho-spiritual rebirth and renewal, perhaps since pre-antiquity linked with the seasons, but also something more. With suicidal tendencies so blatant in the world, this is a perfect moment for a little good, a little birth. It doesn't have to be all or nothing, all at once. A good part of the human spirit is having a rough time but it's still there, coming through all kinds of arrogant truths, lies and scorching fictions. At the same time, there is deep, sharing fiction that expresses truth of feeling, emotional truth, and gives us a sense of the possible in the face of harrowing living deaths. Rosh Hashanah, called the "birthday of the world," more than symbolizes awakening, a birth that never stops, new beginnings, it tries to give some aspect of this ever-growing moment in its service. It does so as fall passes into winter when metaphorically we may need hope most.

In "Shame" (2016, p. 72) Peter goes through a dark version of this moment. He says, "I dreamt a door closed." If a door closes can opening be far behind? Can something open just a little if not now in some distant future? Hope springs eternal but in some moments there seems to be no hope, no way out or, as Sartres writes, "No Exit." One of the basic dualities, counterparts: opening-closing, part of the way bio-systems and emotional life work, a basic rhythm that can get damaged. Our nervous system underwrites this process, as nerves take turns firing and recovering. Opening-closing, firing-recovering. Kaballah speaks of rupture-repair. Melanie Klein emphasizes the importance of reparation in the face of destructive tendencies. So many writers phrase it in somewhat different ways, broken, damage, healing, wholeness. The words recovery and resilience have recently become popular. But some people complain that they cannot heal, that they are broken, damaged and not repairable. Bion writes of contrary emotional "forces," in extremis an ideal sense that can't be destroyed and a destructive force that destroys everything.

When I would read about Newtonian and Coulomb's forces of attraction-repulsion I wondered about the ways everyday experience and science feed each other. So often science seems to be describing emotional states, forces, gravitational pulls, attraction, repulsion, charge – a world of feelings. Worlds collide, worlds interact and nourish each other. When Peter dreamt a door closed and he was locked out of his apartment this very real, everyday happening gave expression to feeling closed or to put it more personally, "I am locked out of myself. I can't find myself. I am locked out of life!"

Peter went on, "All the apartment doors in the hall were blind eyes. I began to disappear." Jesus spoke of eyes that do not see, ears that cannot hear. French poets wrote of emotional or psychic black holes before physics elaborated the term. Do black holes have archetypal meanings? The door locked. Blind eyes. I began to disappear. "I fought to stay alive but it was no use." Were the blind eyes also a mother not seeing her infant, or child, or growing being that she gave birth to? A baby not seen who could not see itself? A baby turning into a black hole, a black hole inside itself and inside the mother? Does one turn into a black hole in order to stay alive?

Psychoanalysis and existential literature depict disappearing in multiple ways. To a greater or lesser extent, we can psychically vanish, go away, lose or be too much for ourselves and develop defenses to save our lives: you can't hurt me if I don't feel anything. In some ways vanishing, disappearing, losing feeling can save us from acute emotional pain, although such operations can end up being still more painful. It can be an awful thing to go through life not being there but for some being there may seem even more catastrophic.

When someone starts getting better their pathology may get worse, at least for a time. Bion wrote of the predicament this sometimes put him in while seeing very ill patients without medical credentials. He moved to Los Angeles late in life, invited by colleagues but lacked California state requirements. He wrote about being fearful he would be sued when a patient got worse on the way to getting better. Freud documented periods when a patient's pathology surged in response to improvement. Often there is a back-and-forth movement that used to be called progress-regress with possible double directional movements: regression for the sake of progression and progression for the sake of regression, creative opposites or, better, creative rhythms. There was, of course, danger that the surge of a destructive tendency or addiction to self-destruction would win out. Masochism-sadism are part of our makeup. Negative energy may become unbound and need reworking, rechanneling, a process envisioned in various forms at least since antiquity. Freud adopted an alchemical term, sublimation, to point to processes where destructive forces can be worked and transformed into constructive energy.

As Peter continued to vanish he felt closer and closer to death. He described his thoughts and feelings as an intravenous drip that went slower and slower. "I thought my brain would die and heart stop beating." He lay on the floor waiting.

I don't want to encourage anyone to do anything to get into trouble and make matters worse, but there is much to be said for a kind of open waiting, a happening I call creative waiting. Freud described a similar open state which Bion depicted as a kind of psychoanalytic faith, a state familiar to meditators. Peter lay on the floor waiting for death – but what kind of death? Perhaps he himself didn't know. Jesus spoke of dying to your self to be reborn, a process that is part of many enlightenment paths. As mentioned earlier, Freud suggested to Fliess that psychoanalysis was akin to ancient mystery cults concerned with psycho-spiritual transformation.

In a way, Peter was stuck in an awful state. Some stuck in such states feel they will last forever or at least the rest of their lives. Yet I feel that sometimes they lead to new openings, a kind of creative waiting on the creative unknown. There are ways of going through these deaths, allowing them, just being, tolerating them, shutting up, going through, don't block it, let the state go where it will. Read Pablo Neruda's "Keeping Still," a celebration of doing nothing, a nothing that turns into a freeing opening. A moment of learning, experiencing a new dimension: Oh my God, maybe I can learn to live with myself in less pinching ways.

Peter somehow opened to surprise: "When I thought my brain would die and heart stop beating I felt less scared." Freud and Jung chart reversals of thought and feeling, sometimes in destructive but also creative keys. I think of a book by C.S. Lewis called *Surprised by Joy* and Bion's adage, "suffering joy," building up tolerance for psychic life in many keys to the extent you can, and then a little more.

This is a paradoxical moment in rebirth literature and practice from time immemorial (for discussion of different kinds of rebirth see Eigen, 1992).

There is a basic renewal process from moment to moment over time. I'm not sure Peter had any choice but to enter it, even if he did not know what it was at work moving him. He had built up enough therapy savoir over time to let the experience unwind and see where it would take him. Perhaps something like a moment saints describe, "Even if you slay me yet I will trust You, love You." Sounds masochistic to some but when it happens it redeems masochism and brings what Emmanuel Ghent (1990) calls "surrender" to another level.

At what seemed like a point of exit that surprisingly turned into a point of entre Peter said, "I thought there was nothing I could do, but there was one thing I could not stop doing. I can experience my own death, at least the start of it or even the middle." Peter seemed to know yet question whether you can experience your own death if you are no longer there to experience it. Can one honestly say or know what's going to happen? I think, too, of Winnicott's prayer, "Lord, may I be alive when I die." Or Steve Jobs reputedly saying "Wow" as he was dying. At that moment it sounds like the "ow" in "wow" let up if not desisted. Or Tolstoy's Ivan Illyich, a character who came alive for the first time at the moment of death. Can fiction have more emotional truth than life?

Peter had intimations he was not actually dying but entering a portal of a kind of psychic death. His resistance to psychic death was lessening, letting whatever it was envelop him, slowly take him over, a taste of death that opens birth. In psychic terms birth gives rise to death and death gives rise to birth, twinships, never one hundred percent, bits at a time. A good deal in life is imaginal, mythic, archetypal. Peter *knew* he would not be there for the end yet waves of death kept coming. Death kept beginning,

Peter was surprised by this kind of beginning, it was not something he sensed before, not so consciously. There was no end to death ever beginning, wave after wave.

Wave is such a basic image for processes, physical waves, electrical waves, magnetic waves, water waves, waves of thoughts and feelings, waves underlying hearing and seeing. Hermetic philosophy speaks of slower and faster vibrations giving birth to different realms of experience. And don't forget we wave to each other as greeting or departure.

Participant: I've been meditating a great deal on creating the mental apparatus. I'm wondering if what you are describing about your patient is part of creating a mental apparatus.

Mike: In a way, what he's doing is creating a less phobic domain about psychic rhythms, dying out-coming back. I wouldn't have thought to put it this way but to use your image, he's creating a psychical, mental apparatus that can sustain its own rhythms.

Participant: And he's going through it without putting an end to it. He's staying open to whatever happens to him, whether he dies or resurrects, dies again, resurrects. Going through it grows the equipment to go through it.

Mike: That's a lovely way to see and put it. Yes, the going through and capacity to go through are growing at the same time. Doing it is giving birth to it. Being with it is giving birth to the possibility of being with it. Putting it in a broader way, less phobic about one's psyche, less phobic about one's experience. It can be awful, scary, all those bad things happening and going to happen. All those scary things are filled with energy.

Participant: In alchemy it's part of a cycle, a cycle that repeats. If you get to the end of the cycle, it starts again. *Mortificado.* It's somehow very helpful to patients to help differentiate between literal and psychological death.

Mike: Right. That's why I used the term "psychic death." One is becoming less phobic about the psyche, a little less phobic about experiencing experience. Bion talks about building tolerance for experience. An important part of what enabled Peter to take a little more of himself, let more of himself in, eg., let deathing and birthing in, is that he has a place to go to share whatever he thinks and feels. Therapy gives him support to begin supporting himself more, let more psyche in, begin better tolerating loss and beginning and so much that may have no name.

Some kind of ability to die out and come back runs through the universe, night and day, nerves firing-recovering, domains of imagining partly weaves psychic experience. For Peter to get sensing-image-thought that death keeps beginning and can be part of beginnings became part of the creative movement of his life.

People say things like keep on going, keep on keeping on. We die. The universe keeps on going, so far. We participate in all kinds of imaginal deaths while alive, as well as creative deaths that open experience. We live with an amazing psyche we are not sure what to do with. So much of its experience is, at least partly, imaginary. So much of what we go through is imaginal. To an important extent, we access our emotional life through attitudes and imaginings. It may be that most of the things we go through we go through in a partial, aborted way. Bits and pieces are important. Perhaps each bit is a whole in itself. But we do access wholeness feelings too which can be helpful and harmful. We keep learning how to evaluate our experience and what to do with it and ourselves, my experience and me, going through life together.

One develops premonitory systems, in part, what Freud called emotional signals. Not just signals of physical danger-safety, pleasure-pain, toward-away, but signals having to do with emotional threat and joy, agonies and goodness. Attitudes and imagination often frame how we interpret experience.

In The Psychotic Core (1986, p. 47) I wrote. "We are hallucinatory beings striving for truth and truth-oriented beings striving for hallucinatory perfection – and the two intermingle in strange ways." We need to respect that we go through things a little at a time and find ways to dose experience out so that we can take, appreciate and use it. It's not simply more of the same but new dimensions keep opening. The Lankavatara Sutra writes of unknown perhaps unknowable transformations that touch, add to, help direct and guide a life. I think of Beatrice in Dante's Heaven surprised that heavens keep opening to more heavens. Of course that can apply to hells too. But it can also apply to moments and possibilities we can scarcely imagine before they happen, openings of life.

Something like that happened for Peter in his own way. Sucked into a hole of shame and somehow gaining. He goes through hells and speaks of jumping into his own reality. Moments of opening he dared not imagine. But don't worry. Days later he exclaims, "Will I come out of this? Will there be anything left of me?" He felt he was in a state of dream-shock and that we were doing "dream-shock therapy."

And the work continues.

References

Balint, M. (1959). *Thrills and Regressions*. London: Routledge (1987).
Bion, W. R. (1965). *Transformations*. London: Routledge (1984).

Blake, W. (1790). *The Marriage of Heaven and Hell*. Virginia Beach, VA: CeeateSpace (2014).

Bloom, H. (1999). *Shakespeare: The Invention of the Human*. New York: Riverhead.

Chardin, T. de (1964). *The Future of Man*. New York: Image Books.

Eigen, M. (1992). *Coming Through the Whirlwind*. Asheville, NC: Chiron Publications.

Eigen, M. (1996). *Psychic Deadness*. London: Routledge.

Eigen, M. (2005). *Emotional Storm*. Middletown, CT: Wesleyan University Press.

Eigen, M. (2015). *Image, Sense, Infinities and Everyday Life*. London: Routledge.

Fairbairn, W. R. (1966). *Psychoanalytic Study of the Personality*. London: Tavistock.

Freud, S. (1926). *The Question of Lay Analysis*. New York. W.W. Norton (1990).

Ghent, E. (1990). Masochism, submission, surrender. *Contemporary Psychoanalysis* 26: 108–136.

Green, A. (1999). *The Work of the Negative*. London: Free Association Books.

Nelson, M. C. (1962). *Paradigmatic Approaches to Psychoanalysis*. New York: Stuyvesant Polyclinic.

Reik, T. (1939). The characteristics of masochism. *American Imago* 1(#1): 26–59.

Reik, T. (1941). *Masoschism in Modern Man*. New York: Farrar & Rinehart.

Spotnitz, H. M. (1968). *Modern Psychoanalysis of the Schizophrenic Patient*. New York: Grune & Stratton.

Chapter 6

Playing With Bion
Gifts and Dreads of Our Problematic Psyche

We are going to play with Bion, a funny playmate with a sense of humor that the phrase "dark humor" does not do justice to. Aspects of his writings really are playful, a kind of play space, which, as for a child, can be a very serious play. Humor, wonder, curiosity. When I sent Francesca Bion, his widow, things colleagues I found interesting wrote, she would say after expressing appreciation, "Oh, I wonder what Wilfred would have said." So I wonder what Wilfred would say about the kinds of things we've talked about and what we will say today. We might even wonder what he would say now about some of the characters in his book. Who are these people? What is their make-up?

But to start off I'd like to mention Bion's *No-Questionnaire* (Ch. 19 p. 89). Today in clinics both patient and therapist often are required to fill out lengthy questionnaires relating to symptoms, diagnosis, biography and other details about the patient's condition and goals. These may not only be for clinical knowledge but for insurance companies, legal issues and reasons not necessarily related to actual clinical work. In the face of this Bion proposes a No-Questionnaire – a situation in which patient and therapist face themselves and each other and begin the business of letting therapy grow. Rather than answer pre-made questions the therapy couple begins a journey toward experiencing what it is like to be together, appreciating growth of contact with one's depths. Not just a matter of filling in the blanks but opening possibilities, perhaps discovering emergent questions rather than knowing answers. Bion's No-Questionnaire is a kind of semi-humorous way of offering appreciation of what might grow from unknowing. A kind of openness related to his formulation of the psychoanalytic attitude being without memory, expectation, understanding and desire. A growing openness to O, unknown emotional reality – I almost said unknown umbilical reality – processes of transformation developing through the work itself, including opening dimensions of experience one might not have imagined existing.

Not quite the same but related, Rabbi Rami Shapiro (2018) proposes translating "vanity, vanity" in *Ecclesiastes* "emptying, emptying," a kind of

DOI: 10.4324/9781032658926-7

open state and method of approach to experience and change. Freud advocated keeping an open mind during sessions, a kind of emptying and readying. He spoke of "blinding oneself artificially" so that the unseen can have an impact – so that, in a way, the unseen can be "seen." Usual judgmental ways of seeing can overly saturate psychic space and act as a barrier to inner perception. It is as though we sometimes need to look out of the corner of our eye, peripheral psychic vision catching fleeting hints of growth possibilities. In this case, I'd like to emphasize the word art in "artificial," an art of practicing a more open seeing, sensing, experiencing. Marion Milner (1987) liked writing Bion's O as 0 (zero), linking it with creative emptiness related to Buddhist *sunyata*.

A No-Questionnaire is a kind of radical openness to the unknown of a session. We don't know what will come next, what may hit us. In a way, all of life is a No-Questionnaire, openness to revelation. Paradoxically, questions are part of it. I find myself asking, "Can you tell me more, say a little more? Do psychic taste buds sense unknown emotional life gestating, reaching for experience?

Donald Meltzer (1976) used to speak of reverie as a way of open sharing. A kind of "here's what's coming to me, I don't know, but does this have anything to do with you? Does it evoke something? Or am I lost in my own autistic moment?" One can rummage through what comes and see if there is something to share. I've heard people say things like, "My mind is stuffed. it seems to have stopped breathing" or "There's no room for me in my own mind." It can turn into its seeming opposite, "My mind is stuffed with stagnant emptiness. My mind has died." A very different kind of emptiness – an implicit generative sense has been lost. Can one wait on one's deadness too?

* * *

A Memoir of the Future is a kind of waking dreamscape, a psychic play space. In Chapters 16–21 voices of dream characters collide, stimulate, inseminate, bypass each other then quiet down and the dreamer sleeps. The dreamer appears to be Roland (Chapter 18, p. 83) but he is part of Bion's dream. It may be all the characters are parts of each other's dreams. And the writer of this narrative or waking-sleeping dream is Bion himself, or the character Bion dreaming Bion.

Whether Roland or Bion (in one of his guises) the lights go out and new characters enter the dream stage – Albert Stegosaurus and Adolf Tyrannosaurus (Chapter 18). I imagine Adolf and Albert dancing, real-life dream characters, a kind of sparring dance, a war between thought and violence? But can't thinking be violent too? Albert throws names at us – relativity – all relative – are we all related? Does anything hold the universe together? "What's that little thing you have," asks Adolf. "A rudimentary brain," Albert answers. In this context, rudimentary is a lot. A lot more than Adolf has?

Adolf warns Albert that a rudimentary brain is dangerous, it can explode and blow Albert's head off (p. 84). It's all too easy to use one's brain against oneself. We've learned a lot about brains but even much is very little. Cortical-subcortical, new brain-old brain, right brain-left brain – intertwining, inter-separating, fusing, melding, opposing – more emotional, more detached, storm-calm. All kinds of combinations. Let me ask, "How's your rudimentary brain doing at the moment?" Our rudimentary brains – curse, blessing, tool, gift, challenge. What a mess – but they're the only brains we've got.

Albert asks Adolf, "What kind of old brain do you have because you sure don't have a new one? Or maybe you use thinking to manipulate and delude – you know how to snow people." One of the great talents of humanity is psychopathic manipulation of catastrophic anxieties in perverse ways. We are or can be dangerous beings.

Adolf confesses, brags, admits that he has a tough unconscious (Ch 18, p. 84). He speaks of not knowing what his right hand is doing. He might as well have said his left and right brains don't know what each is doing, huge dissociative tendencies. I think of the Kabbalah Tree of Life and *Chesed* and *Gevurah* not knowing what each is doing (Eigen, 2012). There are or can be massive dissociations and dislocations in life. One might even come to love violence and the pleasure of inflicting pain rather than be burdened by empathic kindness. A tough unconscious indeed – like a tough inner hide free of the pangs of conscience.

Yet Adolf in trying to insult Albert stumbled on a peculiar seed of wisdom. "It will take you a few thousand years till your concepts cease to be blind and your thoughts without content are discovered by a thinker without thoughts who has room for a few thoughts who can't find a thinker to give them room." (Chapter 18, p. 84).

How is Adolf insulting Albert? He portrays Albert's brain as empty, blind, thoughts without content, no room for a real thought that counts. Maybe in a few thousand years …

But wait a minute – Adolf sounds a lot like Bion speaking of thoughts without a thinker and vicissitudes of birth – psychic birth, mental birth or to coin a phrase by Mary Henle (1962) the birth of ideas.

Is Bion Adolf and Adolf Bion in some way we might hesitate to appreciate? Or is it a bit of Bion's humor, at once light and dark that turns the insult "empty-headed" into something to be desired rather than avoided. If only we could be more open to experience some thoughts searching for a thinker in psychic space for thousands of years, if only some might land and impregnate us. A boon or catastrophe or both – a catastrophic boon akin to a big bang birth of a universe, a mental universe (Bion, 1970).

This reminds me of a passage in *Macbeth* Bion mentions. Macbeth asks Lady Macbeth's doctor, "Can't thou not minister to a mind diseased?" The doctor answers, "For this the patient must minister to herself." Bion adds his own "answer": "Come back in two hundred years and we'll see what we can do."

* * *

Adolph reminds Albert that he, Adolph, has Tyrannosaurus teeth and can chew Albert up and spit him out. Albert reminds Adolph that he, Albert, has Stegosaurus armor. "You fool, don't your realize my armor will wear your teeth out? You're going to break your teeth on my hide and chew your own teeth." Teeth as weapon, armor as defense, teeth as defense, armor as weapon, back and forth, double tendencies in our personality. Sounds like psychological work is needed, more learning and growing to do. Adolph is convinced he can chew and destroy Albert's armor; Albert is convinced his armor is stronger and can destroy Adolph's teeth. Sounds like we're caught in destructive delusions.

Defense vs. Weapons, both functioning as ways to wound and win. On the other hand, there are ways they may work together. I think of a scene from a play my son, Jacob Eigen, wrote – Osama bin Ladin and George W Bush doing a kick dance together. I think, too, of Mom saying to the baby, "I'm going to eat you up. You're good enough to eat." A very different moment from her Tyrannosaurus aspect threatening to chew the baby up and spit it out. Yum-Yuck. Both play a role in survival yet can turn against each other and do more harm than good – how to work with tendencies that can oppose and nourish each other.

Among double tendencies Freud speaks of is aggression turned against the other and aggression turned against the self. Hating other-self can go together, a dual dynamic tendency. Affective movements often undergo fusions and reversals. Adolph may try to chew others and even succeed but at some point reverse and chew himself as well. Or perhaps he began by chewing himself and found ways to direct self-hate outward. We are made up of double-directional tendencies or, better, tendencies that can be multi-directional, including unknown directions yet to be or which may never be discovered. In some ways, we are still mining and feeding off domains Albert's imagination opened. Perhaps he was one of those in whom some "thoughts without a thinker" alighted (e.g. Wertheimer on Einstein, 1945).

* * *

I'd like to backtrack a little to the State Psychiatrist (Ch 17, p. 81) who immediately precedes Adolph Tyrannosaurus and Albert Stegosaurus aspects of our psyche. When I see the words State Psychiatrist I think of my interview for a psychologist job at Rockland State Hospital when I was in graduate school. I failed to get the job and when I asked why was told some thought it odd the way I smiled at the patients. The clincher was going under a bed to talk with a patient who stayed there. Was that too familiar too fast or simply too odd, as I was told? I remember Anna Freud did that.

The first we learn about the State Psychiatrist (p. 81) is that his job is to keep order in the hospital. Bring on the medication, keep the patients calm. I'm not an anti-medication person, far from it. Meds can be terrifically helpful and some of my patients have been on them for decades. And many weaned themselves, wanting to feel what they feel, go through life without them. But here Bion has the State Psychiatrist said, if it's his life or mine, better a patient be drugged so that no one attacks or gets attacked. I can't help thinking of another kind of order – ordering food – what would you like for dinner tonight? Would you like to eat one of your patients for dinner or spit them out? If the patient is too violent we can put him in a little room, lock the door and put his food through a little hole in the bottom of the door.

What would it be like to say, "Order in the Courtroom" to begin a therapy session? Is a therapy session like a court trial and/or anything but? What about ordering or bossing someone about? When we think of order we might also think of chaos. What kind of order did God intend to create out of chaos and nothing in the beginning of Genesis. What kinds of beginnings are possible? Is it a matter of intention or spontaneous happenings, both and factors we don't know about?

One of many good fortunes was getting my doctorate in the school Max Wertheimer taught at for ten years before his death. Gestalt psychology was still alive and well several generations later when I was a graduate student six decades ago. I'm thinking of a particular phrase or aspect of a much larger body of work – how form, structures, systems arise from spontaneous self-ordering of the parts. In this case order is not imposed from above but is self-generated, like the ordering of the solar system or circulation of nutrients by our blood. Gestalt was a kind of field theory in which forces could affect each other at a distance, an issue that vexed Newton and is still developing. The image is less a monarchy-slave model than parts spontaneously organizing themselves in relation to each other, a kind of implicit, intrinsic process. Nevertheless, can't we say that force fields exert intrinsic pressure for parts to organize themselves the way they do? We are made up of forces that limit and make us possible. And creativity is part of the brew. Mystery, puzzles, problems continue and exert their own kinds of pressures. Gestalt liked speaking of different kinds of gaps exerting pressures to be filled in.

Participant: Gestalt means "to shape" in German. Maybe the name has to do with what you are talking about now, like forms occur from within.

Mike: Formation of gestalts can work in various ways, not simply imposed externally or from the top down. Another thing I like in gestalt psychology is talking about incomplete gestalts. There seems to be a force or pressure to complete a gestalt and make it whole rather than live with incompletion and learn more about processes at work. We may jump to conclusions that shut out further possibilities. At times a force to make a whole out of an incomplete gestalt can be delusional.

Participant: Maybe that tells about the January 6th people and the vaccine.

Mike: Say more.

Participant: I don't know. If we do not stay with the incomplete and just want to complete it they have absolutes – absolute answers, pre-answers ...

Mike: Even if they are false – "I'd rather know what's going on even if it's false." The power of belief appeals to a strong organizational tendency. It may not be easy to live with incompletion but that is part of our situation.

Gestalt psychology has many experiments showing how even at the level of perception we tend to fill in gaps and complete an incomplete picture, a tendency to make perception of images or objects more whole than they really are. If this applies to perception you can guess ways to apply to thinking and attitudes (e.g., Wertheimer's essay "On Truth" in Mary Henle's *Documents of Gestalt Psychology*, 1961). I'm an incomplete gestalt made up of many incomplete gestalts.

Participant: I'm thinking of Bion's "selected fact." Waiting on a chaotic pattern, then somehow a selected fact triggers a gestalt, a pattern of organization. This could be a positive variation to the January 6 version, a paranoid process completing a gestalt.

Mike: That's a good distinction, plus and minus completion. A paranoid "completion." Bion puts a double arrow between Melanie Klein's paranoid-schizoid and depressive positions: $Ps \longleftrightarrow D$, a movement back and forth between bits and pieces and depressive "wholes." It's as if Bion gets suffocated by depressive completion and moves back to bits and pieces. A kind of psychic rhythm that in a way mimics catabolic-anabolic tendencies, breaking apart – coming together, somewhat similar to Freud's breaking apart and building unities. You're suggesting that the splitting mechanism can create a kind of paranoid unity, which plays a huge role in psycho-social life.

The State Psychiatrist (p. 81) mentions Newton who could not physically explain how objects affected each other at great distances, so posited God as the force that held the universe together. Order could be a military order, a parental order, all kinds of ordering processes – including paranoid ordering processes. What kinds of order does God create, does a notion of order pertain to God?

Participant:	I'd like to add to what has been said so far with a quote from *The Psychotic Core:* "The struggle for truth is played out against and permeated by hallucination. Notions of lying and falsehood must be rewritten in a hallucinatory key. Freud's work is part of a wider cultural movement in which human beings imagine themselves as coming out of an age-old hallucinatory state; at least this is envisioned as a possibility as a wish."
Participant continues:	The January 6th people were exploited by an inability to differentiate reality from fantasy or hallucination from reality. The Jan. 6th people believe they are coming out of a hallucinatory state into a clarity awakened state that gives them the self-righteous need to act.
Mike:	That reminds me of when I saw Donald Meltzer speak at the 1975 International meeting in London with Andre Green, Leo Rangell and Anna Freud. Meltzer (1976) talked about the "delusion of clarity of insight." That seems to fit with what you are saying. Also, Meltzer calls the reversal of good and bad or truth and falsehood a perversion.
Participant:	I was thinking of the same paper.
Mike:	All kinds of order. All kinds of disorder. Disorder can be creative disorder. For a while the term "creative destruction" used to be popular. Creative disintegration. WInnicott's creative unintegration can overlap with Milner's creative emptiness, akin to *sunyata.*

What kind of order is the State Psychiatrist's? More like policing? But then something of a radical shift occurs. Bion (the character) uses the term "Transformations," as if making fun of himself, alluding to a book he wrote called *Transformations.* And lo and behold, the State Psychiatrist goes through a radical shift – if only therapy could be so easy. The State Psychiatrist free associates a cultural melange, condensations of authors and thoughts and says, "Why, even *I* am transformed." (Ch. 17, p. 81) It is as if the State Psychiatrist is having a session with Bion. Bion used the phrase "breakdown, breakup, breakthrough" a number of times in his writings.

It now looks like the State Psychiatrist is partly going through something like that. On the one hand, rigid order, on the other, schizophrenic word salad, and now transformation. He seems to be saying his very *I* not just his *me* is undergoing transformation. Suddenly, the State Psychiatrist's orderly mind is transforming into the psychotic order-disorder of his hospital patients and yet, perhaps, something further, a genuine shift in his mental culture.

What kind of psychoanalytic order is there in a session? Remember, Bion tells us this whole book is akin to a psychoanalysis or a psychoanalytic session. A psychoanalytic dream, a dream of psychoanalysis. He wants us to feel and appreciate the multiplicity and complexity of psychic reality. I suddenly imagine a mad analyst saying, "I order you to free associate" and then, "I order you to disassociate."

"Why, even *I* am transformed." Even *he*, spokesperson for order in the courtroom can undergo profound change and appreciate aspects of psychic amazingness. A few words by Bion and a sense of psychic possibility deepens. Quite an intervention. If *he* can be transformed, anyone can. "Even *I*." If there's hope for transformation for the State Psychiatrist who didn't like me to smile at (with) the patients, who didn't like me to go under the bed with them, there may even be hope for *me*.

Not a bad little job being a therapist, a psychoanalyst, or whatever we are now, building capacity to be receptive to undergoing and partnering transformation processes, whatever that means. Some transformations are aided by age alone or in partnership with fruitful practices. What a difference it is to be 86 than 23. So much has opened, dimensions I had no idea about and if I did have an idea then the actual happening now is different, freeing. I'm thinking, too, of people for whom only the negative is real and positive aspects of affect and life are felt to be hypocritical – people stuck in the negative. There is much to be said for so-called negative affect and attitudes. They are charged with much energy and can be extremely useful. People have been talking about using or transforming the negative for thousands of years. I like Andre Green's book title, *The Work of the Negative* (1999). The negative in life spurs us to further growth or can lead to suicide. Freud's use of the alchemical term "sublimation" touches on the challenge of turning bad to good, at least in part. So much that can go haywire in us was likely useful at some point of human existence for tool-making and survival. It is a thread, too, to in religions and spiritual practice. There is no one rule or practice. I remember a time in my life when I got tired of staying with the negative and learned to swerve a little: "That's enough, I've gone through enough." Enough for now. Let's swerve a little and make room for some other things. Learning how to swerve or even dissociate can be life-enhancing, sometimes life-saving. There is such a thing as creative dissociation too. So many capacities can be used so many ways. What enables you to live now? Be very careful because live has lie in it – but it is so much more.

I've had many dialogues and interactions with the shadow side and am thankful I read Jung's formulation of it when I was young. I did my senior thesis in college on *Ulysses* and can't help seeing many resemblances in *A Memoir of the Future*. Joyce's daughter had sessions with Jung but it did not keep her out of hospital for much of her life. In a way, too, *A Memoir of the Future* is a living hospital with much verbal medicine to help those who need and can use it.

There are many benefits to being a therapist if one can remain open to the work. I've told the story about my first clinic job seeing patients in individual therapy, part of a training program. After about six months the clinic director calls me in and asks how's it going. "I don't know about the patients," I answered, "but I'm sure getting something." To which the director surprisingly, benevolently replied, "As long as someone's getting something." After training and more supervised experience I taught and supervised there over fifteen years, a very rich background. I used to joke that therapy is for the therapist. One is involved in daily, hourly, moment-to-moment transformation processes. One must be involved – steeped in – dark processes but they, too, become gateways for something more, worlds of psychic beauty that keep opening. I'd almost like to coin the term "crazy beauty" to touch nooks and crannies that lurk around the corner. Why did Saint Paul say it's a dreadful thing to fall into the hands of the living God? One might say the same of the living psyche – home of horrors, promises and moments beyond belief.

As noted above, even the State Psychiatrist is surprised by the shift from being a psychic policeman whose job is to keep external order to one undergoing transformation processes wherein even his I is transformed, his very I. From that moment he becomes sensitive to all kinds of affective nuclei sandwiched together in seemingly endless ways. (p. 81)

Even *I*. Yes, even us – can you feel it, touch it as it touches you, dip in, and in lucky moments even swim. In the rest of this passage State Psychiatrist indeed swims in the psyche and psyche swims in him.

We join him in his discovery: "I am transformed by the work we do." The work is self-transforming and mutually transforming. Even I. Even we. We spoke of different kinds of order, invisible psychic shapes, self-ordering processes. All "parts" of psyche are creating orders and being created by them by spontaneous activity. Spontaneous organizations may come and go like the angels God creates for a moment's work. Others can be longer lasting and undergo development. As Gregory Bateson (1979) says there is always "news of difference." A wonderful thing about a tree is it stays in the same place yet every part expresses changes, leaves, branches, roots, trunk breathe deep change. Tangles of roots thrill me. Can I say as I pass through a day I reorganize just the same way? Moment to moment, hour to hour? There are ways I do not reorganize the same way. Can I actually say I went through a day and am exactly the same as when it began? Did I somehow escape or forestall anything unfamiliar about myself? Or can I, must I say there is invisibly felt difference somehow, for better, worse or beyond such categories. Again and again and again ...

We are brought to a point that goes deeper and deeper – the need for psyche. Phyllis Greenacre spoke of the artist's love affair with the world. There are ways we can say that M. Klein, Winnicott and Bion had love affairs with the psyche. A deep need for psychic contact, surfaces and depths. Awful things can happen. Melanie Klein's daughter could not say enough bad things about her and her son died falling off a mountain. But she also played a role in enriching the development of Winnicott's and Bion's psychic contact, exploration, development and sharing. There is such a thing as being lonely for the psyche and psyche being lonely for us.

We return to the State Psychiatrist's (p. 81) free association cultural rap, mentioning author after author, hinting or touching multiple emotional nuclei, amalgams of horrifying violence and fathomless beauty, spectrums of kaleidoscopic possibilities that characterize experience. Newton, Shakespeare, Jesus, Homer, tiny nibbles fused together giving expression to dilemmas we face with our makeup (I don't mean cosmetics but the ingredients of our beings). Samplings of awful things we do and are as well as filled with wonders. You can be sure Satan says hello as well as all the Cains, a sideways glance at Agamemnon and the work of Time, a kind of giddy mind salad.

We'll pause and dally with Newton a moment or two. State Psychiatrist begins his cultural associations with Newton's mind-mint condensation. To be master of the mind and its riches and/or master riches of the Royal Mint – mind vs. money or simply mind-money fusion and interplay. Newton was appointed head of the Mint and rejuvenated it. So many riches – wisdom, mental riches, emotional riches, sensory riches, financial riches and their tensions and interweaving.

As you know, Newton was a genius physicist-mathematician and as you may or may not know an alchemical Adept. Add to that astronomy, theology and economics. He was perplexed as to how mechanical forces worked at a distance and postulated God holding the universe together enabling distant causation. Future physicists-mathematicians would develop field theories with intrinsic natural forces. One might call Newton a renaissance man, giving expression to many capacities that worked with and against each other. Newton, like the State Psychiatrist, was into order but the order of the universe, not just a mental hospital. And through his various pursuits and explorations underwent transformations as well.

As the State Psychiatrist meanders along, his mind or psyche or being does not seem quite at ease with mechanical order. Life keeps evading it – or is it death that is chimerical as well. Jesus is a nuisance. Why? His spirit evades mechanics? His Presence supersedes it? Macbeth says, "We have scotched the snake not killed it." Can the snake refer to our evil inclination?

To a mercurial aspect of life? What is the snake that keeps nibbling at us? It's not us nibbling at the apple, it's the snake nibbling at us. Macbeth is talking about an enemy dying but the threat lives on. One cannot tame the dog of life. Whoops – apologies, god backwards?

As I quoted before, "Canst thou not minister to a mind diseased?" Macbeth asks the doctor about Lady Macbeth's state. Is mental illness another attempt to break through the prison of mind? What doors does psychosis open? So many Cains in the world. So many murderers in Shakespeare and life. Is there a link between murder and madness or is killing a constitutive element in its own right? Is murder another attempt to break through barriers? (Eigen, 2010; Gilligan and Richards, 2021).

Another theme State Psychiatrist falls into has to do with deadness, being dead while alive, feeling dead. There are many variations. It was a theme that permeated French existential writings (e.g., Camus, *The Stranger*) and French psychoanalysis spoke about what it called an "operational person-ality," people functioning, even functioning well (e.g., heads of government) but lacking feeling. Loss of feeling (e.g., "schizoid personality") was an important area of work and study in British psychoanalysis and writings. State Psychiatrist again thinks-dreams of Shakespeare's language to help out: "Stone death had no fellow." After which he immediately thinks of murderers in Macbeth – as if murder is a way to feel enlivened. Think of Gide's *Immoralist* to begin the 20th century and killing to break through deadness. Self-murder or as Schreber called it, "soul murder" (Eigen, 1986 Chapter 7). I don't mean literal suicide, but what psyche can do to its emotional life in order to survive. A deadness T. S. Eliot returned to again and again, e.g., "The Waste Land" (1922) and "The Hollow Men" (1925), expressing part of an aftermath of the World War. Bion himself confessed that he died in the Battle of Amiens (August, 1918) when he was twenty-one. Human deadness-aliveness became one of the compelling themes throughout his life's work. I have to wonder which can be more destructive the life drive or death drive? So much war and violence seemingly tries to affirm one's own life drive at the expense of others. State Psychiatrist continues to assemble nuances of what psyche is up against, difficulties inherent in its own nature, difficulties inherent in the kind of life form we are and the kind of world and universe we live in.

Murder as a way to break through barriers, including a kind of self-murder to break through oneself, the oppressive trap of oneself and more. State Psychiatrist alludes to Shelley's "Adonais" and how the "rosy hue" of life "stains the white radiance of Eternity." The window of life we value so much itself becomes oppressive, a pain stain. Murder as a way to stay alive, a link with Being? An attempt to break through Being? What does that give us? What does that make us?

Self-perception takes us farther. There are tendencies within undergoing transformations that turn murderous energy into a need to build. In the Bible story, Cain becomes a builder of cities. The same energy that kills, builds. There are ways we are always undergoing transformation, for better and worse, Cain and Abel builders of psyche to this moment.

In *Cogitations* (1991) Bion writes about "truth cruelty" and "truth compassion". While one might like to picture them as worlds apart there are moments a hair's breadth separates them and times nothing does. So many intriguing accidents of language touching currents of life, e.g., truth has ruth in it and life has lie.

Bion can't help mocking humanity by having State Psychiatrist proclaim that murderers have hearts of gold (p. 81), "stout fellows all." Is this all a bad dream, a silly dream, a crazy dream, nightmare-daymare? "Suffer the little children to come unto me with gently smiling jaws." What is going on here? Where are we? What is happening? How?

Two chapters later (Chapter 20) the scene will shift to a detective story. Sherlock Holmes, Watson, Mycroft, and the character called Bion will be a big part of it. Years ago psychoanalysis was looked on as a detective story, solving the crime of personality, symptoms hints of what went wrong, a quest for hidden "causes." Indeed, Freud remarked to Fliess that psychoanalysis was akin to the ancient mystery cults working with transformation processes. One can't help feeling Bion is parodying himself, psychoanalysis, humanity, a kind of psychoanalytic Jonathan Swift.

A murderer turned into a builder. Sounds a bit like Freud's sublimation or Bion's "making the best of a bad job." One way Freud housed these double tendencies was positing a life drive and death drive, the former building, the second breaking apart, partly modeled after anabolic-catabolic tendencies, ingredients of psychic metabolism. What is really happening we may not know but metaphors help us touch and express moments of our lives. We still are very much in process of wondering what to do with ourselves, how to partner varied and complex capacities. To some extent we remain like a kid playing with blocks, building up, breaking apart, rebuilding, learning something about starting. We are very much still at it, in there pitching. How do we use life well or well enough and continue to learn, grow, appreciate and open with both our problem-solving mind and sense of mystery.

References

Bateson, G. (1979). *Mind and Nature: A Necessary Unity*. New York: E. P. Dutton.

Bion, W. R. (1970). *Attention and Interpretation*. London: Routledge, 2013.

Bion, W. R. (1991). *Cogitations*. London: Routledge.

Eigen, M. (1986). *The Psychotic Core*. London: Routledge, 2004.

Eigen, M. (2010). *Eigen in Seoul Vol 1: Madness and Murder*. London: Routledge, 2019.

Eigen, M. (2012). *Kabbalah and Psychoanalysis*. London: Routledge.

Gilligan, J. & Richards, D. A. J. (2021). *Holding Up a Mirror to Nature: Shame, Guilt and Violence in Shakespeare*. New York: Cambridge University Press.

Green, A. (1999). *The Work of the Negative*. London: Free Association Books.

Henle, M. (1962). *The birth and death of ideas*. Eds. H. E. Gruber, G. Terrell, and M. Wertheimer. *Contemporary Approaches to Creative Thinking: A Symposium Held at the University of Colorado* (pp. 31–62). New York: Atherton Press.

Meltzer, D. (1979). *Sexual States of Mind*. London: Phoenix Publishing House, 2018.

Wertheimer, L. (1945). *Productive Thinking*. New York: Harper.

Wertheimer, L. (1961). On truth. Ed. M. Henle. *Documents of Gestalt Psychology*. Berkeley: University of California Press, 2020.

Chapter 7

A Bit of Madness

Bion and Myself have a number of long conversations. As the back and forth go on who is who often blurs. In general, Bion seems to be more the generalizing-thinking-observing mind and Myself an inner associative presence, closer to the experience itself. But a statement like this doesn't always hold. Characters blur into each other yet remain distinct at the same time. One of the biggest blurs is between the actual author himself writing this book and the "fictional" characters his imaginings create and address. Fiction expresses emotional truths of many kinds. Bion has often said that Falstaff is more real than many actual people he knew and in these pages, through the character Myself, affirms that artistic communication is often more accurate than non-artistic methods (p. 110).

It's pretty common to say something like, "I'm talking to myself." Here the I is the character Bion and as may happen in real life, Myself talks back. Myself becomes or is a subject too and perhaps even links back to Plato's describing thought as inner dialogue. A conversation with oneself and the dramatis personae of one's psyche. And sometimes conversation becomes drama.

Bion and Myself are, partly, discussing the nature of the psyche and how to access it. Word patterns, regroups, shifts of tone, color and what they can represent about mind, perception and sense yet something elusive and real escapes them. A presence beyond or in the reality they represent remains somehow beyond representation. A kind of paradox in which language gives rise to a sense of presence that language does not encompass. The unspeakable and speaking in some ways give rise to and develop each other. It is said that something is lost by words at the same time words point to, express and even create a presence of the loss. Words sometimes create new experiences as well as carry a sense of the inexpressible.

I'm thinking of moments when, in my teens and early twenties, basics of the sky, branches of a tree, shadows of the leaves eased tensions in my core that spread through my body and sense of being. As if for moments life's tensions dissolved in life's beauty and the beauty felt deeper.

DOI: 10.4324/9781032658926-8

Dimensions deeper than "core" opened, a moment not only of "wholeness" but freedom from myself.

There's something about sensation, feeling, perception that seek and elude words at the same time. They play a role in making life feel worthwhile yet cannot exhaust a sense of something deeper, ineffable or, as Bion and Myself seem to say cannot be formulated. And maybe here the word "formula" is important. What in us appreciates "a felt sense," that cannot be formulated?

What is it in the experience and actual happening and work of psychoanalysis that can't be formulated? What is it that eludes capture? Perhaps using the word "it" is too much, even though Groddeck (1923) wrote of a kind of "Cosmic It." What is it that eludes mental capture – a funny kind of question since the mind itself is so mysterious and eludes itself. Can we say we have a self-elusive mind? Is our very self-elusiveness part of why we fasten so tightly on bits of identity, socially, personally, religiously, scientifically, culturally derived? Bion and Myself wonder what it is about the actual happening of psychoanalysis that psychoanalytic theory can't capture or do justice to? Are there ways psychoanalysis may be a poetic experience, psychoanalytic poetry or, more broadly a form of art?

There's something about the presence of sensation life, feeling life, emotional life that takes precedence. We think about it – what was that, what did I see, feel, sense? We make up a name. Bion sometimes uses the phrase, "whatever it is" for a sensed, nameless presence.

Often there is war between nameless presence and words, sometimes even between felt perception and words. Bion talks about delineating patterns and configurations that indicate "underlying reality." "Indicate," suggest, not capture. There are more than moments when there is a huge war between writing and words. What is it we are trying to give expression to with the words we use? Does the latter ever evoke the reality it tries to share, delineate, grow from? The very meaning of experiencing can be elusive. What kinds of worlds and meaning do processes of writing try to open? Our patterning and configuring – even the DSM – tries to say something about perceptual, emotional non-verbal worlds the human mind cannot formulate or even conjecture. Bion used the word "conjecture." Freud used constructions, hypotheses. Einstein spoke of imaginings that grew from vague images and body feels partly translated into physical-mathematical terms. What was he plugged into? What was he giving expression to with his mind and very being? Stuff he thought of about stuff that's really there, whatever it is. Remember Eddington's famous statement, "Something unknown is doing we don't know what." But look what we can do with it – and what we can't.

Do we have an inner X-ray machine? Many X-ray machines? Does psychoanalysis, in part, function something like an X-ray machine picturing opaque patterns that have long existed becoming semi-visible through sensitive plates of personality? Our sensitivity to an ancient psyche picturing itself today, this moment, always partial through ongoing conjectures. Myself depicts psychoanalysis as a crude, ephemeral avenue of access touching "forces on the surface of which the human race flickers, flares and fades in response to the unrecognized but gigantic reality." (1991, p. 112). How does one explore the psyche itself, not just the methods (like psychoanalysis) investigating it? Can one get from the method to the thing itself? Myself caps off his longish monologue (Book One, Chapter 24, pp. 110–112) with a statement well known to many Bion fans: "Psychoanalysis itself is just a stripe on the coat of the tiger. Ultimately it may meet the Tiger – The Things Itself- O." Are you ready for this meeting, longing for it, hungry for it, terrified? I think of a line from Buber, "All real living is meeting."

Why Tiger, not hands on the Elephant? Recall Bion's depiction of tiger hunts in India when he was a child and the cry of a tiger whose mate was shot. Broken hearts and souls are not simply priorities of humans. Not to mention William Blake's *Tyger Tyger Burning Bright* and the primal energy it expresses.

What is this x-ray machine inside that is tuned into our emotional life? What kinds of pictures is it taking? Almost sixty years ago I read Herbert Read's *Icon and Idea* (1965) in which he feels image precedes idea in the West by two hundred years. In some ways, image gives birth to ideas, as Einstein depicted as part of his own creative process. One could ask, too, what gives rise to the image? The formula sensation gives rise to image gives rise to idea has its restrictions but also value. Relationships between capacities can be so intricate.

At times Plato seemed anti-image, for example distrusting the verbal images of poets. He favored ideas that he portrayed as incorporeal and called them "Forms." He did not mean visible form and for him "formless" did not seem right either. Perhaps today we could think of them as formative, akin to creation and existence of meaning. But he seemed to think of them as timeless, the most basic being the Idea/Form of the Good. We seem to have a taste for the incorporeal as well as the corporeal. Mystics speak of union with God in which the Good Itself touches a sublime soul, a timeless, ineffable state. It's a state that gets around. To be a little crass, recently I passed two cars next to each other in a driveway, one license plate had an abbreviation of "Be Here Now," the other "Heaven." My mind instantly put together something like: Heaven is here now. I thought of Jesus's "Heaven is within you." And Bion affirming an ideal state that survives and perhaps informs everything. I can't help thinking of Susanne Langer's (1942) depiction of tribal ritual dance as a kind of embodiment of this state, although it may seem a bit odd to speak of embodied incorporeal states. But many think, as Bion does, that multiplicity-complexity is part of our makeup.

My Mom used to speak of finding a balance, advice given long ago in philosophical emphasis of "the middle way." Freud spoke of too much-too little stimulation, flooding-vacant. In the 1960s we spoke of turning on-off, like electricity. Our "sensitive plate" is other than a plate and not just exhausted by the notion of "machine." Our sensitivity can take us many places in many directions. Winnicott spoke of the value of extreme states but also emphasized the importance of moving between, transitional experience, a notion he may have gotten from Martin Buber and amplified his own way. We are sensitive and insensitive in so many ways. A notion of "affect regulation" has become popular. Sounds like a machine or legal model. Would self-modulation be any better? It's no easy matter to become partners with our sensitivity and learn how to be with ourselves, seemingly a never-ending quest and, believe it or not, not just agony but pleasure.

Do you know where your sensitive plates are? Can you feel them? We are sensitive all through our bodies. Sometimes I can't help picturing cellular life as sensitive, sensitivity of our pores as well as emotional and sensory sensitivity. Sensory sensitivity may be where the word "sensitive" developed from, For centuries philosophers wrote about pleasure-pain. It may have been mystics, poets and later writers of fiction that put a spotlight on agony and joy. Crucifixion-resurrection is a kind of archetypal representation of going through agony to joy in its myriad forms, spontaneous movements between good-bad feeling and more. Portrayals of leaving slavery for freedom show other, related facets. It is often said we are slaves to ourselves, our own slaves. There are disciplines and myths about transcending, overcoming, or otherwise becoming freer from self-slavery. Freud likened psychoanalysis to ancient mystery cults that emphasized transformation of states from death to immortality or, simply, worse to better. There are many kinds of deaths and moments of opening and growth in life. Our sensitivity can evolve, even stimulate or create evolution. Straus (1966) suggested how our upright posture grew from an inner urge to enlarge our visual-mental field, in some way physiology following experience. In this case sensitivity stimulates organismic growth, inchoate urges pushing evolution and the physiology to support it.

Bion depicts psychoanalytic portrayals of personality or mind as a kind of recent photogram of a long-existent reality (1991 p. 112). Psychoanalytic mind taking pictures of its insides, our insides. What is taking pictures of what? How? And to add Freud-Bion's picture of transformations, how this becomes that and that becomes this. Mind or personality taking pictures of itself – is that just an image, a metaphor? Freud frequently compared this with that metaphorically. Metaphor not only reflects, expresses but also creates realities. Bion's work adds to psychoanalytic creativity, enhances appreciation of psychoanalytic beauty and possibilities.

By the time we uncover an ancient photogram, we do so from a somewhat different place. By the time we find ways to represent ourselves, other generations are taking their own pictures. We can't keep up with ourselves. By the time we develop pictures of one moment, we are already somewhere else. We may enjoy photos of our psychic insides and learn from them even though the next moment is already seeking attention. By the time we represent ourselves, there are new ways to represent ourselves, new generations of experience and representation.

I deeply appreciate Hegel's dialectic, thesis, antithesis, synthesis that breaks more open, or Winnicott's and Tao's paradoxical experiencing and Bion's counterparts. Processes keep processing. We are more than the sum of our representations. We sense-feel ourselves and ask, "Who am I?" And more opens. We take ourselves by surprise – *it* takes us by surprise. When I look at Renaissance paintings I see the soul or life force in people's faces. In addition to physical forces, Bion speaks of psychic forces, religious forces. His work is implicitly informed by field and quanta theories. One thinks of mathematical and other forms of abstraction in physics, surprised to see how close they can be to everyday experience. Attraction-repulsion and magnetism, for example, are part of everyday phenomenology. Gestalt psychology speaks of force fields that can work at a distance, influence patterns of perception and many variations of experiential organization. It may seem bewildering how influence can work across space and time. Even speaking of "forces" known and unknown seems steeped in human interplay. I hear a child or adult saying, "You forced me to do it, " or "Something forced me to do it," or "Some kind of force or pressure stops me from doing it." Force as a term in war, childcare, crime and creativity and much more. The kinds of things forces do in science, abstruse as they may be, can seem and be very intimate. I've heard people ask to be forced into doing things they wanted to do.

Bion seems to speak of unknown forces rather than drives, although the term force appears on many levels and in many dimensions. A sense of the unknown adds limitless depth to existence. Hearing so much about the unknown and unknown forces the character Bion asks Myself how he can still be practicing psychoanalysis if the latter is linked to and grows from the unknown and in some sense remains an unknowable reality. What kind of science can this be, psychoanalysis as unknown working with the unknown. Perhaps psychoanalysis is a form of poetry or art. Bion delineates the psychoanalytic attitude as F in O, where O is unknown reality and F is Faith, an open attitude and state hypothetically described as being without memory, desire, or understanding – radical openness to unknown emotional reality in the session.

Bion's formulation reminded me of Winnicott's "use of object" paper (Eigen, 1981), moments in which an infant gives spontaneous expression to feeling and the mother receives it openly, supportively surviving the baby's energy in good ways. It seemed to me a kind of intrinsic faith in baby and mother were at work.

Bion (1970) felt important and useful as a medical model can be, it was not sufficient for psychoanalytic realities, in which elusive, ineffable, intangible experience works. How do we register, sense, feel psychic realities that may not be accessible in usual ways? We can learn a lot about the way brain, nerves and organs work but important as this is, they are not our feelings. Psyche is much more than measurements.

"Myself" (1991, p. 113) responds to "Bion's" challenge by comparing himself to a fictitious character. And what bursts out is a sense of how so much fiction gives expression to emotional truth. Shadowing Plato he speaks of an inaudible inner dialogue between "me and me," fearing if such a dialogue became audible it would sound mad. He depicts a double or even triple fear, that the inner conversation and reality it expresses would sound meaningless or worse, that multiple feelings about the same facts would sound mad. How insane must an analyst seem to speak of so many realities and meanings dancing on the head of a pin?

Is the author, Bion, implying that all the fictitious characters he is "creating" are him and/or parts of personality tendencies and self-states? Incomprehensible, imaginary, realistic – different moments of being, nuances of aliveness, challenging bits of life growing in mostly unknown ways from unknown sources? Do conversations in sessions share in this unknown creative and too often destructive life-giving madness? I think, too, of Meltzer (1983) late in life petting and feeding his loved horses and suggesting that what he shares with patients are not "interpretations" but reveries. Reveries that may grow out of confounding realities/possibilities linked with the unknowable.

What Freud says about the id – that the law of contradiction does not hold – Bion applies to psychic work generally, as it appears to be rather pervasive. It seems more the rule than exception that we can have multiple thoughts about the same problems – and "same" in some ways keeps changing. Multiplicity is one of Bion's signatures. Klein, WInnicott and Bion are among those who worked deeply with psychotic registers. Once one catches on one can be sane-mad in productive life-giving ways. I think, too, of Chogyam Trungpa's (2001) term "crazy wisdom." Is there a psychotic dimension in wisdom and vice versa? How many places can the mind be at once – is it always somewhere else? Given current talk about gender should we call God "They" rather than "One" or "All" or whichever touches a moment. It's easy to think one is mad when mind speeds up, slows down, floods, empties, goes here, there, everywhere, anywhere, nowhere.

Bion (1991, p. 113) simplifies the situation by having "Myself" say the analyst may appear mad by having two opposite ideas or sets of feelings about the same "fact." Thoughts may be confused with reality and feelings felt as mad. "Myself" suggests that analysts should get used to being thought mad as it is part of their calling to see and experience multiple possibilities of psychic flow and rigidity. A person may, at times, feel welcome relief to have another presence in the room to partly absorb and acknowledge this situation. Then again, when I think of Piaget describing and contrasting egocentric and decentering modes of thought I think how "normal" seeing things from one and/or multiple points or view can be.

Is there a bit of madness in the room, too much sanitizing sanity? What is me, myself and I doing? While Bion was in New York in 1977 I went to his seminars, talk, party and two private sessions. One of the themes of our sessions was building tolerance for the psyche's multiplicity, what you're feeling and not feeling, support the growth of psychic experience. When I walked into the room he was using for therapy we both stood by the door. He was taller than I by far. We were looking at each other and a feeling I had related to the word "understand," to stand under. In some way I felt he was standing under me to support my relationship to my psyche, being and life grow – to help *me* grow. At the same time I felt or imagined I could see his wound, vulnerability, strength and share of *chochma* (potential to be, wisdom bits). Socrates called himself both a gadfly and mid-wife but here with me was a real human being and we were in it together.

In the section of A Memoir of the Future (Chapter 24) I've been talking about how "Myself" lets "Bion" in on what is going on between "me and me." Bion the author is saying it is a function of the analyst to support the patient's ambiguity. He is thinking, in part, of a letter by Keats in which the poet writes of the importance of tolerating ambiguity "without irritably reaching after facts and reasons." This goes along with building up tolerance for oneself, one's states and possibilities, working with what one can. Sometimes seeing the madness-sanity of the analyst helps one tolerate, experience and support one's own. Being with the analyst helps one become less phobic about one's own psyche and perhaps also the psyche of others. It is important to have someone in one's corner to talk to about what can't be said or heard. Someone to be with in a psychical way, who values psyche-talk. A paradoxical result of mutual psyche talk and experiencing madness-saneness together is growth of self-support, capacity to work with one's capacities in fuller ways. Am I too sane, too crazy? I'm something that doesn't fit that – something else. I don't know what this something else is but I can feel it, sense it. It's amazing. Amazing Grace? Amazing Life? Amazing Psyche? Amazing O?

References

Bion, W. R. (1970). *Attention and Interpretation*. London: Routledge.
Bion, W. R. (1991). *A Memoir of the Future*. London: Routledge.
Eigen, M (1981). The area of faith in Winnicott, Lacan and Bion. *Int. J. Psychoanal.* 62:413–434.
Collected in Eigen, *The Electrified Tightrope* (1993). Ed. A. Phillips. London: Routledge.

Groddeck, G. (1923). *The Book of the It*. New York: Random House, 1961.

Langer, S. (1942). *Philosophy in a New Key*. Cambridge, Mass: Havard University, 1996.

Meltzer, D. (1983). *Dream Life: A Re-examination of the Psychoanalytic Theory of Technique*. London: *Phoenix*, 2018.

Read, H. (1965). *Icon and Idea. The Function of Art in the Development of Human Consciousness*. New York: Shocken Books.

Straus. E. (1966). *Phenomenological Psychology: The Selected Papers of Erwin W. Straus*. New York: Basic Books.

Trungpa, C. (2001). *Crazy Wisdom (Dharma Ocean)*. Boulder, Co: Shambhala Publications.

Index

For Product Safety Concerns and Information please contact our EU
representative GPSR@taylorandfrancis.com
Taylor & Francis Verlag GmbH, Kaufingerstraße 24, 80331 München, Germany

www.ingramcontent.com/pod-product-compliance
Lightning Source LLC
Chambersburg PA
CBHW070349270326
41926CB00017B/4056

9 781032 674308